"Ron Hiebert is the Warren Buffet of Alberta. Read this book and reap the financial rewards."
Randy Marshall
CHQT radio personality

"I co-wrote Making Money the Old-Fashioned Way, *a book on basic investing, with Ron. Everything he said in 1993, about steady, value-oriented investing, building wealth one step at a time ... has unfolded in my own investment portfolio exactly as he said it would. His excellent financial guidance has stood the test of time."*
Graham Hicks
Columnist, *Edmonton Sun*

"Ron Hiebert has done what few authors have done. He has succeeded in writing an investment book which is full of valuable investment advice, yet easy to understand."
Gary Coskey

Wealth Building

Proven Strategies
To REALLY Make Money

Also by Ron Hiebert
(co-authored with Graham Hicks)

Making Money The Old-Fashioned Way
– sensible investing for personal financial security

Wealth Building

Proven Strategies To REALLY Make Money

BY
RON HIEBERT

Published by
ELRON Enterprises
Edmonton, Alberta

Canadian Cataloging in Publication Data
Hiebert, Ron, 1953-
Wealth Building — proven strategies to REALLY make money

Includes index.
ISBN 0-9686108-0-3

1. Finance, Personal. 2. Investments. I. Title

HG179.H53 1999 332.024'01 C99-901387-4

Published by:
ELRON Enterprises
Edmonton, Alberta

Acknowledgments

The author would like to thank the following individuals for their assistance in producing this book:

Melinda Peacock,
Carol Hanna,
Dave Hiebert,
Silver Hiebert (the dog),

Bowes Publishing Ltd.:
Elsie Rose, Don Sinclair, Dennis Stankov, Nicole Stusek-Soroka,

Jasper Printing.

DEDICATION

To my family
Penny, Nicole, Barrett, Brendan, Brock

CONTENTS

PREFACE

Wealth building strategies that work

Wealth building is the latest buzzword. But it's really more than that. Wealth building represents many things to many people. Sufficient financial assets is a cushion you can draw from in times of trouble, a nest egg that can assure a comfortable retirement or a reserve that can give you the flexibility to take time off during your career, or leave a job you don't like to launch the career of your dreams. We're not talking *just* money. Rather, people want what money can buy. And they like the security of being financially independent. Money equals freedom and choice.

The baby boomers are beginning to focus on the need to invest for retirement. Many of us fear the eroding of government programs such as OAS and CPP and reduced benefits or coverage under employer sponsored plans. Individuals shouldn't rely exclusively on government to take care of future needs. Every individual ought to take charge of his or her financial future, now, to ensure a comfortable, financially secure retirement.

Many people believe that building wealth is difficult, time consuming, and only for those with much education and financial savvy. This is simply not true. This book offers a practical, hands-on approach to building wealth. By following these seven steps anyone can easily reach his or her financial goals.

Step 1 — Wealth building requires experience

Over the years, I have interviewed thousands of successful investors. None of these people had a get-rich-quick philosophy. Rather, they built their wealth by the slow and steady accumulation of quality assets over time. Very seldom did these wealthy individuals become so by inheritance, brilliant speculative investments, superior intelligence or even luck.

It doesn't take a Ph.D., a Master's degree, or even a high school degree to acquire financial success. Consider the example of Lilly Wong. Penniless Lilly, who never completed elementary school, struggled with learning English when she came to Canada. She had to provide for eight children when her husband died. Yet, working at the family's grocery store she did so well that Revenue Canada insisted that she pay $225,000 in back taxes for interest earned from Canada Savings Bonds. Lilly only invested in Canada Savings Bonds, unaware that interest was taxable. With her CSBs worth over $900,000 Lilly did remarkably well, despite her circumstances, and the unpaid taxes.

Making money isn't a haphazard process. It requires a systematic, disciplined approach. *Wealth Building — proven strategies to REALLY make money*, outlines an easy-to-follow method for reaching financial goals. You can become financially independent through solid planning, hard work, frugality and patience.

Step 2 — Wealth building requires a plan

To achieve wealth, you must have a plan. What are your goals, plans and aspirations? What do you want to do and why? Take stock. After you have a picture of where you are and where you want to go, you can design a plan to get you to your destination.

Step 3 — Wealth building requires knowledge

Wealth building requires that you become an active participant in the pursuit of your financial goals. You should thoroughly understand the financial tools that can be used to help you reach your goals. A treasure chest of financial information is available to anyone interested in wealth management. Numerous books, seminars, courses, newsletters, magazines and consultations with financial professionals can provide insight and education on choosing financial tools and incorporating sound financial strategies into your portfolio.

Step 4 — Wealth building requires a consistent investment strategy

After developing a financial road map, it's important to assess your tax situation, tolerance for risk and current assets and liabilities. After determining these factors, an appropriate asset mix and investment strategy can be implemented.

For example, if you're a very conservative investor, you may want to consider the following breakdown:

- 20 percent in short-term interest bearing assets;
- 50 percent in bonds;
- 30 percent in preferred shares.

If you're more aggressive and have a large tax problem you might opt for a different mix:

- 10 percent in short-term interest bearing assets;
- 20 percent in bonds;
- 30 percent in domestic stocks or mutual funds;
- 30 percent in international stocks or mutual funds;

• 10 percent in tax shelters or limited partnerships.

Asset mixes come in as many shapes and sizes as individuals themselves. Make sure yours is a good fit to your wants and needs.

Step 5 — Wealth building should maximize returns and minimize risk

Your ultimate goal is to achieve maximum returns with minimum risk. In a fixed income portfolio, this strategy involves buying high quality bonds and preferreds with a good credit rating and then adjusting the maturity of the portfolio in response to changes in interest rates. When rates are low, the portfolio should be seeking short-term investments. As rates rise, the terms of the bonds being purchased should be lengthened to lock in higher yields.

Establishing a margin of safety is even more important when purchasing stocks. The best way to achieve this is to use very rigid criteria in the stock selection process. Then stick to it, religiously. Historically, a value oriented approach offers the best returns with the least risk. Stocks that qualify need to have low levels of debt, be priced at or below the value of their underlying assets, pay an attractive dividend, and have a low price to earnings multiple (P.E.). In addition, they need to dominate the market sector they are in, or be a monopoly. The less competition the company faces, the more profits they will make.

Once a stock is selected and a purchase is made, then time is the most critical factor. To achieve satisfactory results, value stocks are normally held one business cycle (between three and six years) before being sold. Aggressive trading typically results in higher transaction costs, more taxes payable (every time a stock is sold for a profit, a taxable capital gain is triggered) and fewer profits because the shares were sold too early.

Since Canada makes up only three percent of the world's stock and bond markets, foreign diversification is critical if you want to reduce risk and increase potential returns. A minimum of 25 percent of your portfolio's assets should be placed in foreign denominated stocks or bonds, using the selection criteria mentioned above. Currency movement adds additional risk, making it important to time purchases so that the international currency being acquired is at a reasonable level against the Canadian dollar.

Step 6 — Wealth building requires constant vigilance
Times change. Needs change. Economic and political conditions change. As a result, portfolios continually need fine tuning to keep them performing at optimum levels. You should conduct a quarterly or semi-annual personal financial review.

Step 7 — Wealth building requires a holistic system
Most individuals who build substantial wealth follow a system similar to the one described above. They establish realistic goals. They develop a systematic plan to reach those goals. Then they learn about and apply superior time tested investment strategies. They monitor their progress and make changes as necessary. This book gives you insights on how wealth building is REALLY created. It shows you proven strategies to REALLY make money.

CHAPTER 1

A WORD FROM THE WISE

- Where the wealthy get their money
- Accumulating the right assets
- Learning from *The Millionaire Next Door*
- How to profit from major economic trends

The greatest good you can do for another is not just to share your riches, but to reveal to him his own.

Benjamin Disraeli

I've got all the money I will ever need if I die by four o'clock.

Henry Youngman

To invest successfully over a lifetime does not require a stratospheric IQ, unusual business insights or inside information. What's needed is a sound intellectual framework for making decisions and the ability to keep emotions from corroding that framework.

Warren Buffet

Where the wealthy get their money

When P.T. Barnum said there's a sucker born every minute he may have been referring to the seemingly inexhaustible supply of people who respond to the get-rich-quick schemes advertised in newspapers and on television infomercials.

In my more naive past, I went to a financial seminar held at a local hotel. The modern day snake oil salesman promised me riches beyond my wildest dreams. When I coughed up $500 to buy his investment course, I would go through time and learn the secrets of the mega-rich, from Solomon to J. Paul Getty.

Like many of these types of courses, the theme revolved around leverage and risk. I was to borrow money and plunk it down on a high risk investment. Unfortunately, the salesman never told me the chances of turning my poke into a pot of gold were about one in a million. Put another way, my chances of losing everything was about 999,999 out of one million.

These snake oil type courses reinforce the erroneous notion that people with money know something you and I don't. Supposedly, when we have access to the "secrets" the rich use, we should be able to quickly and effortlessly accumulate large sums of money.

Thankfully, a large body of research debunks the myth that wealth can be obtained without effort and over short periods of time. A study in *Private Asset Management* magazine, 1995, examined 879 individuals with liquid assets of $400,000 to over $10 million. This study, and many others, gives us information about who the wealthy are and how they got that way.

Notably, 64 percent of the respondents were between the ages of 50 and 64, while another 18 percent were over 65 years of age. Together they accounted for 82 percent of the group. Wealth comes with age, because for the majority, asset accumulation is a slow process over a long time.

Education was another key factor. High school graduates represented 22 percent of the group, university or college graduates represented 59 percent, while another 19 percent had completed various levels of graduate studies. None of the respondents were drop outs. This study shows a high correlation between education and wealth. There is much truth to the old saying, "the more you know, the more you make."

The marital statistics of the group also present some surprising numbers. Individuals still on their first marriage represented 67 percent, 16 percent had been married more than once, nine percent were divorced, six percent were widowed and two percent were never married. The stereotype of the rich and single playboy or playgirl doesn't mesh with the statistics, as only two percent of the wealthy individuals were never married. Statistically speaking, the people who had the best chance of becoming wealthy were involved in long-term marital relationships.

The source of wealth is also interesting: 54.6 percent came from a business owned by the person or his immediate family; 22.8 percent came from the earnings of a professional practice such as law or medicine; 6.7 percent came from inheritances; 5.5 percent from corporate employment; 5.3 percent from real estate investments; 5.1 percent came from other types of investing. Three quarters of the respondents became wealthy through the ownership of a business or being in professional practice. As anyone who has tried knows, neither of these routes holds the promise of getting rich quick.

This study duplicates the findings of many others. As a rule, the wealthy are generally older, committed to a long-term marriage relationship and have post secondary education. They have made their money over a long time through their own business or professional practice.

Not surprisingly, this smacks of hard work over a long time. These true secrets of wealth will never be revealed in a pricey get-rich-quick course.

Accumulating the right assets

Every man is the architect of his own fortune.
Appius Claudius

Wealth building involves acquiring enough assets during an individual's working years so he or she has enough money to replace working income upon retirement. Crossover, when a portfolio makes more money for an investor than he or she can earn from working, is considered the benchmark among financial planning types. Most people need to reach crossover before they can achieve true financial freedom.

Unfortunately, most retirees never reach crossover. While assets are accumulated, they aren't the right kind. To achieve a financially secure retirement, assets that grow into greater profits are the best bet.

Assets for play

A popular poster "Justification for a Higher Education" pictures an enormous mansion on a cliff overlooking an ocean. Parked in the five-car garage is a Porsche, Ferrari, Mercedes, Rolls Royce and a BMW. The message: wealth is recreational toys. Whether it's a car, boat, stereo, computer or skidoo, these assets depreciate. The average car loses 50 percent of its value over five years and 90 percent over 10. New stereos and computers are worth 50 cents on the dollar when taken out of the box. Some 12 months later, when technologically obsolete, they are landfill candidates. These are depreciating assets, with their value diminishing to zero. While you might have fun with these kinds of assets, they won't do much to move you toward a financially secure retirement.

Assets for show

Due to their rarity, some things can become more valuable with age. Antique cars, coins, furniture, paintings, jewelry and even vintage wine can be included in this category. If you're extremely knowledgeable, the collectibles you pick might even retain their purchase price. If you add a bit of incredible luck, and hold them long enough, their value might even increase. Collectibles are considered a break even asset.

Assets as insurance

As insurance against the ravages of high inflation, many people prefer owning hard assets like gold, raw land or a personal residence. Historically, the appreciation of these assets has closely mirrored the increase in the cost of living. However, since inflation is expected to remain fairly docile well into the future, the long-term growth rate of this asset class will probably remain between two and four percent per annum.

Assets that grow

The secret to wealth creation is a consistent long-term strategy of investing capital in assets that recycle your money into more profits. These assets include stocks, bonds, mutual funds, loans, rental property and small business. Crossover can only be achieved when the bulk of an investor's capital is placed into wealth building assets.

The one with the wrong assets is the loser

In a painting called "The Meaning of Life" a heap of personal assets like stereos, cars and paintings are piled on top of a gravestone. The caption at the bottom of the picture says, "the one with the most assets wins."

When it comes to retirement, the opposite is true — the one with the most "wrong" kinds of assets doesn't win. In fact, he or she loses out on a financially secure retirement.

Learning from *The Millionaire Next Door*

Most people never become financially independent because their preconceived ideas on how the wealthy got that way border on fantasy. It's tough to become monetarily self-sufficient if you don't have a clue how wealth is really created.

This almost universal ignorance on how millionaires got that way was one of the major reasons why Thomas Stanley and William Kanko co-authored the book *The Millionaire Next Door*. The authors, both Ph.D.s., have studied the lifestyle habits of affluent Americans for more than 20 years. During that period, they found who the wealthy were and who they were not. Most importantly, they discovered that the average person can easily duplicate the manner in which the majority of millionaires acquired their wealth.

Contrary to what Robin Leach might tell you on "Lifestyles of the Rich and Famous" most millionaires share the following characteristics:

- most don't live in upscale neighborhoods;
- most drive modestly priced domestic vehicles;
- about two-thirds are self-employed;
- 80 percent are first generation millionaires;
- 91 percent were never gifted even a dollar's worth of the family business;
- 95 percent own stocks;
- most live well below their means;
- the majority wear inexpensive clothing;
- 62 percent know their monthly expenses;
- most do not actively trade their investment portfolio;
- 97 percent are homeowners;
- 50 percent have lived in their present home for over 20 years;

- most allocate considerable time, energy and money towards wealth building;
- the majority place a far higher value on financial independence than status;
- the average millionaire is 57 and married with three kids;
- the average millionaire makes $130,000 per year and is worth $1,600,000.

The book paints the picture of average individuals who became financially independent through solid planning, hard work, frugality and patience. Very seldom did the wealthy become so by inheritance, brilliant speculative investments, advanced degrees or even luck. Anyone can follow this road to riches.

The Millionaire Next Door is a continuous bestseller. It is a must read for anyone wanting to know how ordinary people can become wealthy. At a price of $30, it is the investment bargain of the decade. Buy one for yourself or give the book as a gift to your children or grandchildren. This priceless information deserves to be on everyone's bookshelf.

How to profit from major economic trends

By understanding an economic trend, you can choose the appropriate investment action. You should be able to identify the trend early enough in its life and then purchase the appropriate investments before the herd arrives and the investment opportunity is gone. This article highlights the six most commonly reoccuring economic trends. With a strategic plan for each trend, you can profit from them as they occur.

Trend 1 — Interest rates start rising

Lock in debt before rates move higher. If you have a mortgage with a six-month term or a floating interest rate, secure your mortgage at a fixed rate for a longer term. If the interest rates on your credit cards are high, consolidate your debts at a lower interest rate, with a fixed term and fixed rate consumer loan. If you have a stock portfolio or equity mutual funds, take some profits, as rising interest rates are usually bad news for stocks. Rate hikes often make the market drop dramatically. Those with interest bearing investments should keep rolling their money in liquid 30 to 90-day deposits or money market funds. Wait until interest rates peak. Anyone who purchased bonds at the top of the previous cycle should consider selling them. The profits made when interest rates were down will disappear when rates rise.

Trend 2 — Interest rates are dropping

This is a good time to have a floating rate mortgage and consumer debt. As rates go down, the monthly interest payments will also drop. Falling rates usually signal the beginning of a new upswing in the stock market. Start looking at buying undervalued shares or adding to an equity mutual fund. Before rates drop, investors with a primary focus on fixed income should purchase bonds or other interest bearing investments with as long a term as they feel comfortable, to lock in the higher interest rates.

Trend 3 — Inflation rates are rising

Higher interest rates often accompany higher inflation numbers. In this situation, you generally want to avoid stocks and not lock in money into interest bearing investments for the longer term. Hard assets such as real estate, precious metals and commodities like oil, wheat, base metals and forest products, generally perform spectacularly in a higher inflation environment.

Trend 4 — Inflation rates are dropping

Generally, lower inflation rates are a harbinger of lower interest rates. In this scenario, selectively buy stocks or equity mutual funds. Lock in interest bearing investments at these higher interest levels. Sell hard assets, as their value drops dramatically when there is no threat of inflation. People with personal debt should keep it at a floating rate. Wait until inflation falls and interest rates drop before locking into a longer term.

Trend 5 — The Canadian dollar is rising against major foreign currencies

In this scenario, it's more expensive for foreigners to purchase Canadian-made goods because their currency buys fewer of our dollars. It's more difficult for our exporters to compete on the world stage because our products are overpriced. Sales suffer and the exporting company's stock drops. On the other hand, companies that import foreign goods can buy more because of the higher value of our currency against others. Since the imported goods now cost less, it usually means more profit for the importer. Thus, its company stock rises.

Trend 6 — The Canadian dollar is falling against major foreign currencies

In this scenario, exports are cheaper and more competitive while imports are more expensive and less appealing. Canadian companies that are exporters should be bought and those companies that are major importers should be sold or avoided.

Now that you know what course to take during any particular economic event, you have won half of the investment battle. When you can recognize these trends early and get there before the herd, you can translate this strategy into a real money maker.

CHAPTER 2

BUILDING AN INVESTMENT PORTFOLIO THAT'S RIGHT FOR YOU

- The investor's challenge
- Choosing an appropriate asset mix
- Understanding the basics of fixed income and stock market investments
- Managing your portfolio

To pull off a great investment coup it is best to be the only buyer of a stock that you're building a position in.

Warren Buffet

I've never been poor, only broke. Being poor is a frame of mind. Being broke is only a temporary situation.

Mike Todd

There's nothing wrong with cash. It gives you time to think.

Robert Prechter Jr.

The investor's challenge

Stocks have been among the best performing investments over the long haul, especially if their rate of return is calculated factoring in the effects of tax and inflation. Professor Jeremy Siegel, in his ground breaking book *Stocks for the Long Run*, demonstrates this conclusively in his detailed research of the period starting in 1802 and ending in 1996. Through that span, US stocks sustained an average growth rate of 5.9 percent per year versus 2.3 percent for bonds and 2.1 percent for treasury bills after taxes and inflation. During that 194-year time period, gold, which many people still view as the ultimate long-term investment, only grew by .06 percent per year. This return didn't even match the annual 1.3 percent rise in inflation. Over the term of professor Siegel's study, annual returns on stocks were 250 percent better than those of bonds, 280 percent superior to those of treasury bills and 980 percent better than those of gold.

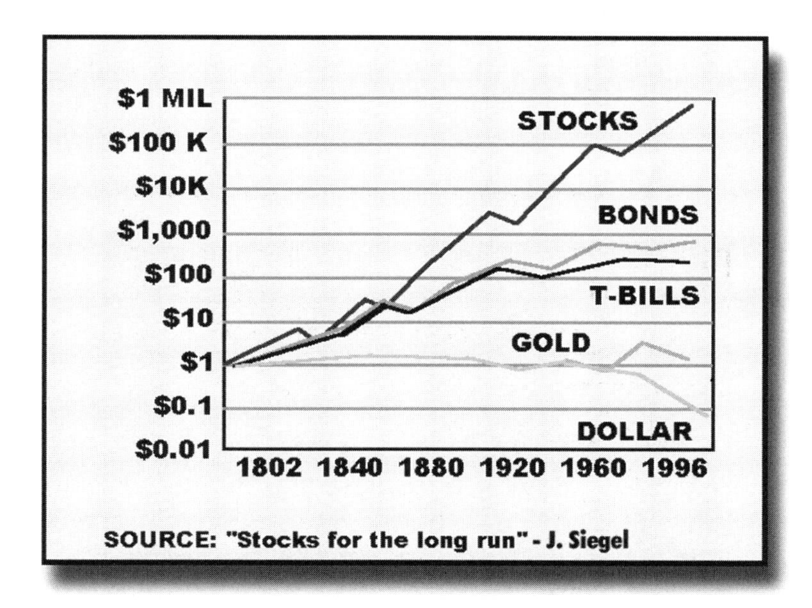

Since the real world returns on equities dwarf those of almost any other asset class by comparison, it's very tempting to put one's entire assets into the stock market. The only problem with this strategy arises when stocks move down. Every decade in recent history has seen at least one significant drop in share prices. In the 1960s the largest pull back, as a percentage, was 35.9. The '70s and '80s had their own problems with the largest market drops registering 45.1 and 36.1 percent respectively.

Not only does the equity investor face the risk of markets going down, but history also shows that they can stay in the tank for extended periods. Witness the performance of the Dow Jones Industrial Average which peaked at 1,000 points in 1969 and then didn't exceed that level again for another 12 years. The Japanese stock markets are another case. They crested in 1989 at 39,000 points. Today, they are trading at one-third of their former highs.

Siegel's research gives comfort to the long-term holder of stocks. He indicates that time is definitely on his or her side and the risk of holding stocks is greatly reduced the longer the securities are held. He shows that in any one-year time period during the two century study, stocks beat bonds about 60 percent of the time. Over any five-year time frame, the odds of stocks beating the performance of bonds grows to 70 percent. For a 20-year holding period the probability leaps to 91 percent. At 30 years, the odds of stocks beating bond investments climbs to an overwhelming 99 percent.

HOLDING PORTFOLIO FOR..	RETURNS			% OF TIMES STOCKS BEAT	
	STOCKS	BONDS	T-BILLS	BONDS	T-BILLS
1 YEAR	4.4%	-1.8%	-1.7%	67%	67%
2 YEARS	9.1%	-3.6%	-3.4%	76%	80%
3 YEARS	13.9%	-5.4%	-5.1%	84%	86%
4 YEARS	18.9%	-7.1%	-6.7%	86%	86%
5 YEARS	24.2%	-8.8%	-8.3%	88%	82%
10 YEARS	54.3%	-16.8%	-16.0%	90%	86%
15 YEARS	91.7%	-24.1%	-23.0%	100%	92%
20 YEARS	138.1%	-30.7%	-29.4%	100%	100%
25 YEARS	195.7%	-36.8%	-35.3%	100%	100%
30 YEARS	267.3%	-42.3%	-40.7%	100%	100%

SOURCE: "Stocks for the Long Run" - J. Siegel

The numbers in Canada are slightly different because of the tepid performance of our stock market in comparison to that of our southern neighbor. However, even during the dismal period between 1969 to 1997, the performance of the stock market on a pretax and pre-inflation basis was still 10.69 percent per year versus 11.34 percent per year for bonds. However, on an after tax basis, stocks managed to turn the performance table on their bond brethren and still be the clear winner.

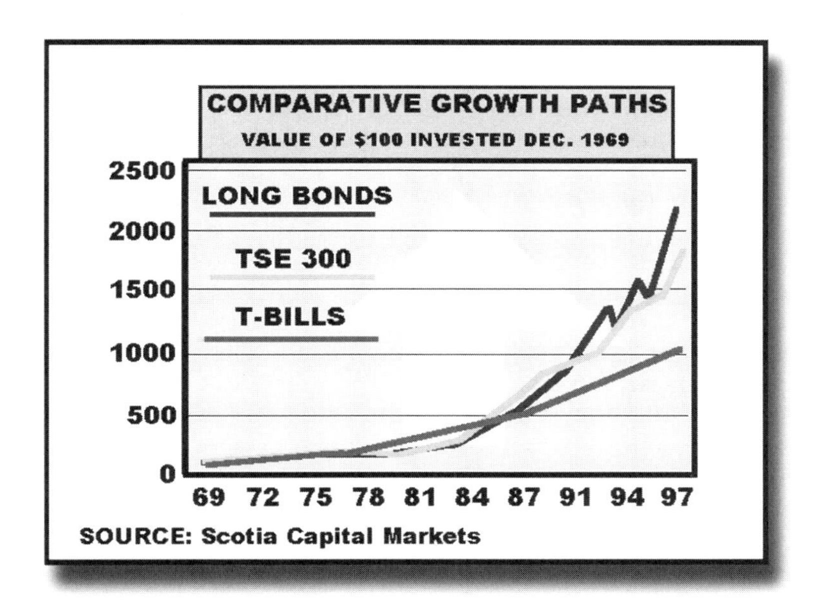

Sidelining the number crunching for a moment, an investor's challenge involves finding an asset mix that allows him or her to take advantage of the overwhelming performance edge that exposure to the stock market brings. At the same time, the investor needs to protect the portfolio should the financial markets take a large fall and then remain submerged for extended periods.

By taking into account factors like age, risk tolerance, current portfolio mix and level of taxation, you can build a portfolio that's uniquely suited to your needs and temperament.

Choosing an appropriate asset mix

Determining an appropriate asset mix for a portfolio is a challenge for any investor. The road to the promised land starts with this philosophy: *Enough exposure to the stock market to take advantage of its potentially higher returns while balancing that premise with enough fixed income investments to minimize volatility and risk.*

Most investors should start with an asset mix of 60 percent stocks and 40 percent fixed income. Thereafter, fine tune these weightings based on age, risk tolerance, level of taxation and need for income. Here's an explanation of these factors.

Age or time horizon

Since younger investors have more time to recover from dropping security values, a higher portion of the portfolio can be devoted to stocks. Conversely, investors at retirement usually need to take money out of the portfolio to supplement part or all of their living expenses. For these people, selling assets when they are reduced in value has an adverse effect on the portfolio's long-term ability to provide income. For the right portfolio mix based on age criteria, consider a percentage equal to age in fixed income securities. For example, a 20-year-old should have 20 percent of their portfolio in assets like treasury bills, GICs, bonds or preferred shares. A 60-year-old should have 60 percent of his or her portfolio in fixed income securities.

Experience

A prudent person (with exposure to equities for at least two business cycles of between eight and 10 years), can place a larger portion of his or her total net worth into stocks. Since a more experienced investor is less likely to make novice mistakes that affect the bottom line, he or she qualifies to reduce the exposure to fixed income investments by 10 percent. Based on the previous rule, a 60-year-old, who has 60 percent of his or her portfolio in fixed income, could reduce the fixed income weighting to 50 percent.

Income and tax bracket

Many individuals do not need income from their portfolio to live. He or she can draw on other sources of income such as pensions, rental properties or an active business. For high income investors, a large cash flow bumps their tax bracket sending too much money to Revenue Canada. Investors with these constraints need the capital gains and tax deferral benefits that come with a heavier exposure to equities. Those in this category can reduce exposure to fixed income investments a further 10 percent. Therefore, a 60-year-old, who has been investing for at least two business cycles and has no need for income or has a high priority to reduce tax, could reasonably commit 40 percent of his or her portfolio to fixed income investments (60-10-10=40).

Risk tolerance

The one factor that supercedes all the others is tolerance to risk. If the price swings that a portfolio experiences in volatile markets leads to sleepless nights, then its asset weighting is probably too aggressive and needs to be conservatively rebalanced. To calculate an individual's (John) sleep point or level of risk tolerance, first determine the amount of dollar loss that it would take to push John beyond his comfort zone. For example, if John had a portfolio worth $100,000 and the most he felt he could comfortably cope with was a drop in value of $10,000, his tolerance to loss (expressed in percentage terms) is 10 percent.

Then calculate John's maximum amount of exposure to the stock market. Let's assume that a standard worst case scenario for the stock market, in any given year, is a 50 percent drop in value. Based on this assumption, no more than $20,000 of John's $100,000 portfolio should be exposed to equities if it's believed that their value could drop by half. Any higher exposure would exceed John's level of risk tolerance, which for his size of portfolio is $10,000. As a percentage, John's risk tolerance level allows for no more than 20 percent ($100,000 divided by $20,000) of the portfolio into stocks. As a rule, the risk tolerance calculation over rides those made for age, experience and income. After all, no amount of money is worth losing one's health over.

Understanding the basics of fixed income and stock market investments

Once an appropriate asset mix has been developed, the next job is to pick individual stocks and fixed income investments for your portfolio.

Fixed income fundamentals

Unfortunately, investments that generate interest income also attract the highest tax. Therefore, before purchasing interest bearing investments consider their placement within a portfolio. Generally speaking, investments facing high tax consequences should be positioned to attract the lowest rate of tax. RRSPs, which offer a tax shelter, are an obvious choice. The investment account of a lower tax paying spouse, child or business can also be appropriate for interest bearing investments.

For those needing tax relief in addition to income, consider preferred shares. Since the cash flow generated from this investment qualifies for the dividend tax credit, there's a lower tax rate. Also consider income trusts issued by utility companies. These investments offer high yields accompanied by low risk and favorable tax treatment.

Deferred stocks are an obvious choice for investors looking for growth, low tax and safety. Deferreds are purchased at one price and then mature at a higher one on a future fixed date. The maturity price is guaranteed payable by the issuing company. Deferred shares are similar to compounding GICs, however, their gains are eligible for capital gains treatment and aren't taxable until the units mature or are sold.

With a fixed income portfolio, the yield or income an investment produces is driven by term to maturity and credit risk. Generally, the longer the term, the higher the income it produces. Investors need to be compensated by a higher rate of return before they become willing to lock money up for extended periods. During periods of low rates, keep investment terms short and due dates laddered or staggered to maturities of not more than five years. Conversely, when rates are lofty, it's more profitable to ladder maturities to favor longer holding periods. By doing so, it's possible to capture higher levels of income for longer stretches.

Credit risk relates to a company's ability to repay loan obligations. The larger the company's indebtedness, the larger its default risk. Before purchasing investments offering extraordinary rates of return, check the issuer's repayment ability. Agencies like Standard & Poor's (S & P), The Dominion Bond Rating Service, Moody's and the Canadian Bond Rating Service rank credit worthiness. When purchasing fixed income investments with inferior credit quality, it's essential to compensate for the increased risk by diversifying wisely.

When building an efficient fixed income portfolio, be mindful of the consequences of tax, term and credit.

Stock market fundamentals

An equity portfolio should be diversified enough to negate the drop in value of any one security. A $100,000 portfolio should have a minimum of eight stocks. Above $100,000, the portfolio should have a minimum of 16 different positions. In an eight-stock portfolio, each section should represent a different industry group to properly diversify. In a 16-stock portfolio, two stocks from the same industry group are appropriate. A portfolio of less than eight stocks gives inadequate diversification. A portfolio of more than 25 stocks is difficult to manage.

Any collection of stocks, adequately diversified by sector, should have representation from the following core groups: utilities; pipelines; banks; financial services; telecommunications; food processing; food distribution; pharmaceuticals; entertainment; medical services; spirits; beverages and household items. A core group represents products and services needed and consumed by everyone on a daily basis — regardless of the economic climate. Core sectors are further characterized by steady and predictable sales and earnings. Investments made in blue chip companies within this group normally experience low volatility and steady growth. The holding period for this type of stock can regularly extend for decades — thus, the term, core holding.

The risk adverse investor, which includes just about everyone, should have a 90 percent portfolio weighting in core holdings. That leaves a maximum of 10 percent of the portfolio allocated to satellite or non-core positions. This non-core group is characterized by higher risk companies with volatile, sporadic and highly unpredictable sales and earnings patterns. This includes technology, mining, forest products, precious metals and energy related businesses. Since the share prices of this group are subject to large swings, buying at the bottom of their cycle and trading out at the top is the only way to make money.

A portfolio should also be diversified geographically to reduce political and economic risk. More importantly, it should maximize potential return. Politically stable first world countries in western

Europe, Asia and North America represent the best candidates. Canada has had sub-par rates of economic performance for decades. This is unlikely to change anytime soon. Considering Canada's dreary outlook, maintain at least 25 percent — preferably much more — in international investments.

Consider your age when selecting individual securities. Those near retirement and requiring cash flow need to purchase stocks with a healthy dividend. Those who are younger or in a high tax bracket would be better off in shares where the gain comes from appreciation in share price. Because taxes are not paid on stocks until they are sold, payment can be deferred for decades. An investor can compound 100-cent dollars instead of 50-cent dollars for many years.

Time to take action

By following these guidelines it's possible to build a diversified, high quality portfolio that gives good returns with only a minimal amount of risk.

How to determine your optimum portfolio mix

Read the following statements.
Agree = 1
Neutral = 2
Disagree = 3

1. I don't expect to need capital or income for my portfolio for several years:

   1 2 3

2. I don't expect my portfolio to provide much current income:

   1 2 3

3. I'm willing to accept some price volatility in return for potentially long-term returns:

   1 2 3

4. I believe the stock market will outperform inflation over the longer term:

   1 2 3

5. I don't currently need a high level of liquidity in my portfolio:

   1 2 3

Scores:

	Cash	**Fixed Income**	**Securities**
13-15	40%	40%	20%
8-12	20%	40%	40%
5-7	10%	30%	60%

Managing your portfolio

The final question to be answered in the portfolio building process is, "Who will drive the bus?" Will you manage the portfolio yourself, farm out the responsibility or adopt a strategy that's somewhere in the middle? Here's a review of the most popular options, each with their pros and cons.

Doing it yourself
Generally, a do-it-yourselfer will hold an account at a discount brokerage firm. He or she will then make investment decisions based on information garnered from financial periodicals, computer data bases, personal research or from a network of other smart do-it-yourselfers. With this approach you rely on yourself for the gains and losses. You also save considerable dollars by being your own guru. The disadvantage: many self-styled professionals have neither the time, personality or aptitude to do a good job of managing the portfolio.

Going half-way
The half-way house is a combination of doing it yourself and seeking assistance from professionals. A fee-for-service planner will develop a financial road map. Then you need to find someone to purchase the suggested investments. Since fee-for-service planners don't make money from commissions on products, their advice is generally considered the least biased.

The second type of financial planner helps you develop a monetary strategy and make investment acquisitions. This category of planner includes insurance agents, personal investment managers at banks and mutual fund representatives. Since these people have considerable experience with individual financial products, their knowledge on the specifics of what to buy is generally better than that of fee-for-service planners. This second group, however, may offer a limited range of financial products. This puts you at a disadvantage if you want to deal with only one individual or institution. This type of planner gets remunerated from sales instead of advice. There may be a bias towards products that pay the highest commissions instead of those which are best for you.

The final category of financial help is generally called an I.E. or investment executive. This person is normally employed by a brokerage firm. Depending on the individual, he or she will either help you develop an overall financial strategy or execute a plan that has been developed by someone else. With this option, you have access to a complete line of financial products spanning insurance, stocks and bonds, mutual funds, tax shelters and precious metals. As it is a fee or commission driven service, carefully discern whether the advice is in your best financial interest.

In some ways, getting help is a good strategy. You can keep your hands on the decision making process. At the same time, professional help is available.

The good and bad of discretionary money management

Generally, this service is offered through the asset management arm of banks, brokerage firms, trust companies and private money managers. To begin the process, you complete a detailed investment analysis. This determines the appropriate asset mix and portfolio structure. Then suitable investment guidelines are drafted and agreed upon by both parties. Thereafter, the portfolio manager has complete discretion to make investment decisions on your behalf, as long as he or she stays within the agreed guidelines.

In this scenario, you don't spend needless time worrying about your money. Your assets are in the hands of investment professionals who charge a fixed fee to do their job.

The downside is the cost. Management fees can eat up between one and three percent of the value of your portfolio every year. Also, except for the occasional meeting scheduled with the portfolio manager or representative, you're isolated from the investment process.

Note: performance studies indicate that the majority of professional money managers are incapable of matching the returns of the major market indices — let alone beat them. This has always been a compelling argument for the do-it-yourselfer. Why not cut costs and increase performance by investing in a handful of stocks and bonds or indexed funds. Then sit on them.

What approach is best for you?

In choosing your money management approach, consider the time you have and your financial skill. The more you have of both, the more capable you are of making your own decisions. Age and health are other factors, especially later in life. Shopping is the only way to know what approach is best for you. Talk to all kinds of financial professionals. Also talk to their clients for a balanced input into the positives and negatives of each kind of service. The amount of homework you do directly affects the quality of your decision. Experiment. If one approach doesn't work, try another. Ultimately, it's your decision and your money.

Your personal investment review

O money, money, money.
I am not necessarily one of those
Who think thee holy.
But I often stop to wonder
How thee canst go out so fast
When thou comest in so slowly.
Ogden Nash

Before you plan your portfolio or seek professional financial assistance, take some time to review your financial picture. Prior to making any financial decisions, determine these two items:

1. Your current financial situation.
2. Your tolerance for risk.

The following worksheet takes you through various aspects of financial planning. The worksheet begins with the basics, ensuring you have a will drafted and that you record names of financial advisors.

In the asset review section, you're asked to list all sources of income, including fixed income securities, RRSPs, stocks and other investments. From there, you'll develop a picture of your overall net worth and your investment objectives.

By asking a few questions on personal interests, available time, risk versus reward, liquidity and investment time horizon, you can then determine the kind of professional help you need, or whether you can comfortably manage your portfolio yourself.

Be sure to list any additional financial information such as health conditions (for yourself or your family), education plans, travel goals, saving for a major purchase, and career aspirations.

Take the completed worksheet to your financial advisor. You'll have a good foundation from which to build your financial future.

Personal Investment Review

Your Personal Profile

Name

Address

City | Province | Postal Code

Telephone Number (Day) | (Evening)

Date of Birth | Social Insurance Number

Occupation | Employer

Employment Income | Other Income | Marginal Tax Rate

Your spouse

Name

Date of Birth | Social Insurance Number

Occupation | Employer

Employment Income | Other Income | Marginal Tax Rate

Do you have any dependents? Yes ☐ No ☐ What are their ages?

Do you have a will? Yes ☐ No ☐ Where is it filed?

Keep a record of the names of your financial advisors here.

Bank | Branch

Bank | Branch

Accountant	Firm
Investment Advisor	Firm
Lawyer	Firm

ASSET REVIEW SECTION I RSP ASSETS

Do you have an RSP? Yes ☐ No ☐ Does your spouse have an RSP? Yes ☐ No ☐

Do either of you contribute to a spousal plan? Yes ☐ No ☐

Are you making maximum annual contributions? Yes ☐ No ☐

Describe the types of plans you and your spouse are holding below.

	Financial Institution, Current Yield and Maturity Date	Reg. Owner You	Reg. Owner Spouse	Approximate Plan Value
Deposits held with *(bank, trust company, mutual fund dealer)*				
Company Group RSP				
Self-Directed Plans				
			TOTAL VALUE $	

SECTION II

Additional Savings Plans ***(at current market value)***

Life Insurance *(cash surrender value)*	$
Company Pension Plans	$
Educational Savings Plans	$
Retirement Income Funds	$
Annuities	$
Other *(include Deferred Profit-Sharing Plans)*	$

TOTAL VALUE $ ______

SECTION III

Personal Property ***(estimated at current market value)***

Principal residence	$
Vacation property	$
Business interests	$
Collectibles *(art, antiques, jewelry, etc)*	$
Other major items *(vehicles, furniture)*	$
Other personal property	$

TOTAL VALUE $ ______

SECTION IV INVESTMENT PORTFOLIO

Fixed-Income Securities	Quantity	Description of Security *(maturity date where applicable)*	Registered Owner You (√)	Registered Owner *Spouse* (√)	Original Cost	Approximate Market Value
for example:						
Canada Savings Bonds						
Term Deposits & GICs						
Treasury Bills						
Money Market Funds						
Bonds						
Bond Funds						
Mortgages						
Preferred Shares						

Stocks						
for example:						
Common Shares						
Convertible Shares						
Equity Mutual Funds						
Warrants						
Tax-Advantaged Investments						
for example:						
Flow-Through Shares						
Limited Partnerships						
Real Estate						
Other						
for example:						
Options						
Gold and Silver						
Futures *(Enclose an additional worksheet if required)*						

TOTAL VALUE $ ______

SECTION V Overall Review of Your Net Worth

Personal Assets

Personal Assets	
Savings and chequing accounts	$
RSP assets (Section I)	$
Additional savings plans (Section II)	$
Personal property (Section III)	$
Investment portfolio (Section IV)	$

TOTAL ASSETS $ ____________

Less Personal Liabilities

Less Personal Liabilities	
Mortgage on home	$
Mortgage on vacation property	$
Credit card balance	$
Personal consumer loans	$
Investment loans	$
Other liabilities	$

TOTAL LIABILITIES $ ____________

ESTIMATED NET WORTH (your total assets less total liabilities) $ ____________

Investment Objectives

The following questions are designed to help you put your financial objectives into perspective. Check or circle the one that best describes your current situation or interests.

Overall Objectives

Select one of the three following that best describes the primary objective of your investment portfolio:

1. Income
   Generate high annual income through dividends and interest with reduced opportunity for growth.

2. Growth
   Value of assets accumulates over the long term with little or no current income.

3. Balanced income & growth
   Blend of capital growth potential and income with low volatility and average returns.

Evaluate the following more specific objectives

(5 being most important)

Reduce income taxes	1	2	3	4	5
Meet future educational expenses	1	2	3	4	5
Plan for retirement	1	2	3	4	5
Provide a hedge against inflation	1	2	3	4	5
Provide for an estate	1	2	3	4	5
Manage risk	1	2	3	4	5
Save for major purchase	1	2	3	4	5

Account Supervision

The role you take in supervising your account will depend on your personal interests and available time.
(Please indicate your intentions)

- Prefer discretionary money management (a professional will make all investment decisions on your behalf) ☐
- Minimal involvement ☐
- Prefer to work with a professional advisor ☐
- Intend to increase involvement with increased knowledge ☐
- Enjoy complete responsibility for account direction ☐

Risk versus Reward

Realizing that there is always a trade-off between high returns and risk, what risk category would you feel most comfortable with?

Preservation of capital very important - no risk ☐

Will accept some risk ☐

Will accept a higher degree of risk for possibility of greater returns ☐

Liquidity

It's a good idea to keep a liquid component in your portfolio to meet sudden cash requirements. What percentage of your portfolio would be sufficient as a liquid reserve?

Need under 20% liquidity ☐

Need 50% liquidity ☐

Need 100% liquidity ☐

Investment Time Horizon

Whether you are investing for retirement or short-term gains, you should determine your investment time horizon.

Short-term: under 1 year ☐

Medium-term: under 5 years ☐

Medium-term: between 5 and 10 years ☐

Long-term: greater than 10 years ☐

Tax Savings

Are you taking advantage of the dividend tax credit? Yes ☐ No ☐

Stock savings plans are available to the residents of certain provinces, and will provide either a tax deduction or a tax credit with the purchase of qualifying shares.

Have you maximized the deduction/credit available to you? Yes ☐ No ☐

Investment Experience

To ensure that you have a complete understanding of all your investment alternatives rate your investment experience.

Excellent ☐

Good ☐

Fair ☐

Nil ☐

Please check any of the investments you are familiar with.

Common Shares ☐	Government Bonds ☐
Preferred Shares ☐	Government Coupons ☐
Equity Mutual Funds ☐	Mortgage-Backed Securities ☐
Warrants ☐	Money Market Mutual Funds ☐
Corporate Bonds & Debentures ☐	Fixed-Income Mutual Funds ☐
Convertible Debentures ☐	Balanced Mutual Funds ☐
Canada Savings Bonds ☐	Other ☐ ________
Government Treasury Bills ☐	

Indicate which special plans you would like more information on:

Self-directed RSPs ☐ | Retirement Income Funds ☐
Home Mortgage RSPs ☐ | Group RSPs ☐
Educational Savings Plans ☐ | Other ☐ ______
Spousal RSPs ☐

Sophisticated Strategies

If you are an experienced investor and you have already established a well diversified portfolio, you may want to advance to more sophisticated investment strategies. If you qualify, indicate your areas of interest:

Stock option strategies ☐ | Commodity futures ☐
Bond option strategies ☐ | Hedging techniques ☐
Index options ☐ | Short selling ☐
Financial futures ☐ | Other ☐ ______

Special Account Services

Do you need?

Full margin facilities ☐
Secure custody of all your securities ☐
Monthly transfers of dividend or interest income to a financial institution of your choice ☐
Reinvestment of dividends for certain stocks ☐
Cash balances in U.S. dollars as opposed to Canadian dollars ☐
Continuous supervision of short-term money market investments ☐

Additional Financial Information

CHAPTER 3

HOW TO MANAGE RISK

- Dollar cost averaging — how to make money in volatile markets
- Lower risk with higher returns — the promise of asset allocation
- Risk is definitely a four-letter word
- Jimmy the Greek and grade six math
- Storm proofing your investment portfolio
- Adding shock absorbers to your portfolio

We go to the movies to be entertained, not to see rape, ransacking, pillage and looting. We can get all that in the stock market.

Kennedy Gammage

Stock prices tend to discount what has been unanimously reported by the mass media.

Louis Ehrenkrantz

Make money and the whole nation will conspire to call you a gentleman.

George Bernard Shaw

Dollar cost averaging — the way to make money in volatile markets

To make $1 million in the stock market start with $2 million.

Wall Street

This joke isn't far off the mark. Statistics show that about 70 percent of those who invest in stocks lose money. This is amazing, considering that, on average, long-term growth in the stock market is about 10 percent per annum. How do so many people lose money in an investment that over the long-term has outperformed almost every other investment class including real estate, bonds and treasury bills?

The investor's psyche offers some answers. Fear and greed, two powerful emotions, often drive investment decisions. Unfortunately, greed causes people to buy at the top of the market and fear pushes them to sell at the bottom. People lose money this way although the long-term trend is up.

Dollar cost averaging (DCA) helps reduce the volatility of the markets and puts more money in your pocket. With DCA you buy an investment on a regular basis with a fixed amount of money and then continue to do this over a long period of time. The following examples illustrate how DCA is a money making tool in volatile markets.

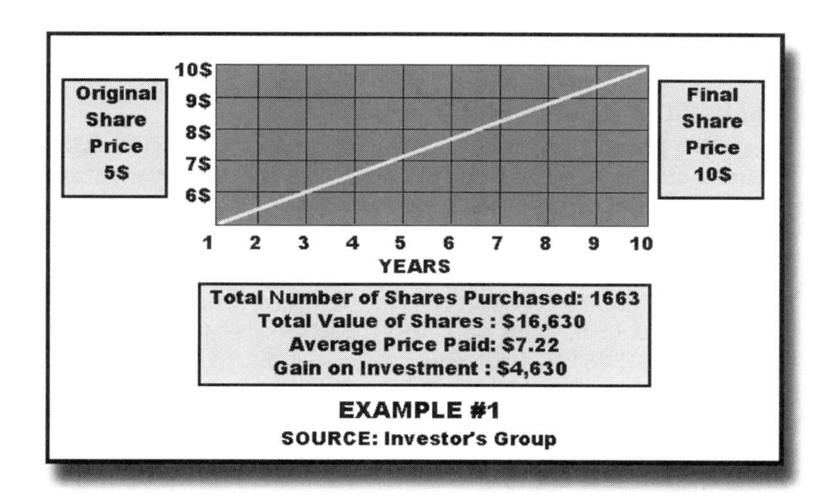

EXAMPLE #1
SOURCE: Investor's Group

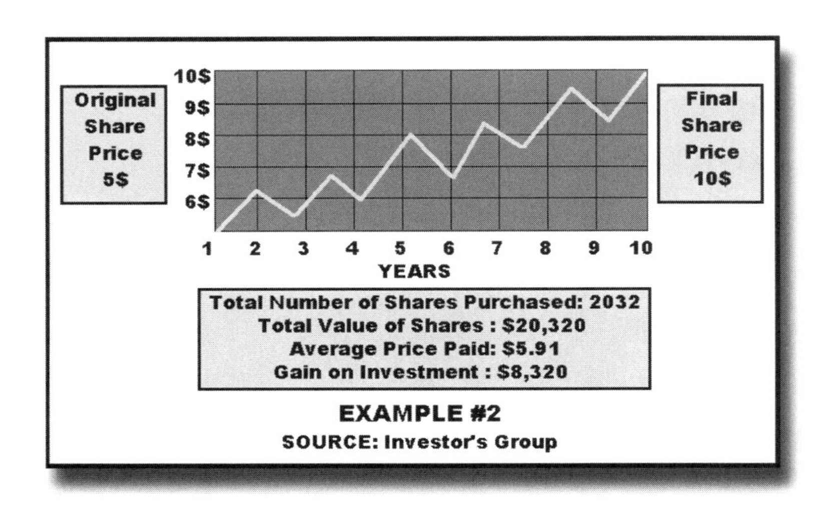

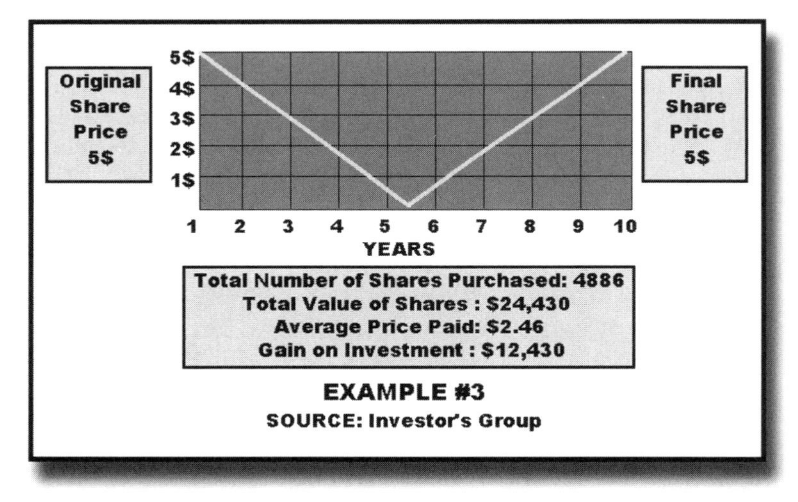

Who makes the most over 10 years?

Investor one puts $100 per month into a mutual fund. The unit price starts at $5 in year one and over 10 years grows in a linear fashion to $10 per unit.

Investor two follows the same plan of investing $100 per month over 10 years. While the unit price of the investment climbs from $5 to $10 per unit over the same 10-year period, the growth path is a jagged line. This saw-tooth pattern sees the fund's unit price go from $3 to $6 and then down to $4 and then up to $7 and so on over the investment term.

Investor three follows the same investment program of $100 per month over the same period in the same investment. The investment starts at $5 per unit. At the five-year mark it sinks in a straight line down to $1 per unit. Over the next five years it climbs back up to the original price of $5.

All three investors put $100 a month into a fund, but under considerably different market conditions. Investor one sees only a gentle rise in the price action of the fund over the 10-year period. Investor two sees the same total rise in his or her fund as investor one does over the 10-year period but with much more volatility during the interim. Investor three sees his or her fund decline by 80 percent over the first five years and then only rise back to its original price by year 10. Which investor do you think had the best return over the 10-year period?

While most people pick investor one, the right answer is investor three. Over 10 years, investor three would have purchased 4,886 shares at an average price of $2.46. The total value of the units would be $24,430, with the gain on investment $12,430. Investor two would have purchased 2,032 shares at an average price of $5.91. The total value of the shares purchased would be $20.321 and the gain on investment would be $8,320, putting investor two in second place.

Investor one would be the poorest, having purchased 1,663 units at an average price of $7.22. The total value of the shares at the end of 10 years would be $16,630 and the gain on investment would be $4,630. In numeric terms, investor three did 2.54 times better than investor one and 1.49 times better than investor two.

How DCA works

Dollar cost averaging often works better in volatile markets rather than in gently undulating ones. In a volatile market, prices go up, but they also go down. Opportunity is born in these down periods. When markets drop, the price becomes cheaper, which in turn means you can buy MORE units of the investment for the SAME price. The more often the markets go down, the more chances you have to buy at bargain basement prices.

DCA works because the long-term trend of the market is up. Over the 120-year period between 1871 and 1990, a one dollar investment in the stock market would have grown, even after subtracting the effects of inflation to $8,192. Viewed from this longer term perspective, the market's movement is a series of swings between higher highs and higher lows.

Therefore, when stocks take one of their frequent kamikaze dives, those people who use DCA, view it as an investment opportunity rather than an investment calamity. These people are getting one more chance to buy cheaply before the next market upswing.

While dollar cost averaging is the best technique for making money in volatile markets, it's also the easiest on your psyche. Who ever thought you would enjoy bad markets?

Lower risk with higher returns — the promise of asset allocation

While everyone wants to obtain superior returns from their investments, few are willing to tolerate the higher risks accompanying these ventures. A strategy that delivers the Holy Grail of bigger returns and lesser risks is "asset allocation."

With asset allocation you assign a percentage of your portfolio to different types of assets including stocks, real estate, precious metals, and short-term and long-term interest bearing investments, to name a few. For example, if a person with $100,000 to invest, divides equally between the five above mentioned asset classes, he or she would put 20 percent, or $20,000 into each asset.

The premise behind asset allocation is that different types of assets perform differently under various economic conditions. For example, when interest rates are low, stocks usually do well, while interest bearing investments give a poor return. When inflation rates are soaring, real estate and precious metal investments tend to give big returns while stocks and bonds are in the tank.

Reduce volatility

Asset allocation usually helps to reduce a portfolio's volatility. Poorer performing assets are usually offset by the better producers. (For a complete study of asset allocation, read the book *Risk is a Four-Letter Word* by George Hartmann.)

From 1972 to 1993, a portfolio of long-term US bonds would have posted a 9.4 percent annual compounded rate of return. Yet, a portfolio of 40 percent US stocks, 40 percent treasury bills (short-term interest bearing) and 20 percent long-term government bonds would have provided the same returns with only 50 percent of the volatility.

While the stock market rose spectacularly between 1925 and 1937, it also fell almost 90 percent during the 1929 stock market crash. During this period, one dollar invested in either stocks or real estate would have grown to about $1.54 over the 12-year period. One dollar invested in government bonds over the same period of time would have become $1.75.

However, a portfolio divided equally among those three asset classes would have grown to $1.87. This balanced portfolio would have outperformed each of the individual ones, with less risk or volatility.

The same criteria was applied to three other periods of time when stocks, bonds or real estate crashed and the diversified portfolio placed first or second in total return and was always the lowest in volatility.

Diversify to reduce risk

Before you can allocate your assets, decide what kind of returns you want and your risk tolerance. Since 1950, treasury bills have averaged 6.4 percent per year, five-year GICs averaged 7.6 percent per year, Canadian stocks averaged 11.2 percent per year and gold grew 4.3 percent per year.

Since some investments are riskier than others, the risk adverse person should assign a greater percentage to GICs. The growth oriented person would overweight stocks and real estate.

Regularly check your asset allocation. Asset classes will grow at different rates depending on market conditions. If the percentage in any asset class is five or more percent off target, consider rebalancing.

You can rebalance with two strategies. Firstly, use new money to buy more of the holdings that are down. Secondly, sell some of the winners and buy more of the poor performers. While this seems rather mechanical, it forces you to sell high (your winners) and buy low (your losers).

Remove the emotional barriers

Since buying and selling are the most emotional parts of the investment process, they are the most prone to error. Taking fear and greed motivations out of the investment decision greatly enhances your performance. Out of fear people sell when the price drops. When the prices are rising, the motive is often greed and they buy. Unfortunately, buying high and selling low is a one way ticket to the poor house.

Asset allocation forces you to take the most profitable, yet least natural course of action (buying low when you are scared and selling high when you are greedy). Asset allocation helps make correct buying and selling decisions, with decreased risk and increased returns. For most investors, it's like having your cake and eating it too.

Risk is definitely a four-letter word

The hallmark of the successful investor is minimizing risk and maximizing reward. To do this an investor must know the types of risk and understand the techniques of neutralizing risk. Here's a review of how various kinds of risk affect your investments.

Business risk
Even the best businesses, with the best management in the highest growth industries, can fail. When you diversify you will not be wiped out by a market sector or economic change.

Quality risk
Risk increases when a company is small, has no established earnings history or has unsustainable high levels of debt. While these companies offer higher rewards, they may drop the most in bad economic times. A portfolio of low quality stocks is a time bomb waiting to explode.

Market risk
Market risk is the general risk you take when you buy an equity. If the stock market as a whole falls, then most individual stocks will also fall. You can offset market risk by diversifying into different types of assets.

Industry risk
Industry risk comes from concentrating investments in a few industries. If a sector is doing badly then the returns on the bulk of your money will also perform poorly. Industry risk can be lowered by holding a portfolio of stocks in a variety of industries such as manufacturing, utilities, banking and communications.

Currency risk
Currency volatility can enhance or reduce the return on your foreign investments. Currency risk can be reduced by focusing on investments in currencies that are low or have recently fallen against the Canadian dollar.

Taxation risk
It's not what you make that counts, it's what you keep. If you're in the top bracket, your taxation rate on securities is roughly:

- one-half of interest income;
- one-third of capital gains and dividend income;

• one-quarter of royalty income.

With high tax rates, it is essential to find investments that lower your taxes or defer payment as long as possible.

Political risk and geographic risk

Avoid a high percentage of investments in any one country or geographic region. Most Canadians incur high geographic risk by having too large a percentage of their portfolio in Canada. Diversification can guard against internal instability caused from high levels of debt and threatened political separation.

Interest rate risk

Bond prices rise when interest rates go down and drop when interest rates rise. Generally speaking, keep your money short-term when interest rates are low and lock in as rates rise. Incorrect timing is expensive. Locking in when rates are low will result in lost yield and a drop in the price of your investment. Interest rates also affect stocks generally. When rates are rising, stocks are going down and when rates go down, stocks rise.

Liquidity risk

Beware of investments with no active market of buyers and sellers. When enthusiasm for a particular investment dries up, you can end up trapped in a security that is free falling. There's no way to get out, because you have no one to sell your investment to.

Technology risk

Due to scientific advances, state-of-the-art technology can become obsolete within months. When investing in a technology based company make sure they have the ability to continuously improve their product or have a pipeline of new ones to replace the one that is obsolete.

Inflation risk

In times of low inflation, financial assets like bonds and GICs perform well. However, in a high inflationary environment, the value of fixed income investments usually gets devastated. In these times, hard assets such as real estate, precious metals and the shares of asset rich companies tend to perform well. Since you cannot forecast inflation, diversify your portfolio with investments that do well in high inflation periods, and investments that do well in times of low inflation.

Risk is ALWAYS lurking in the shadows. Without making adequate provisions for it, risk will always be a four-letter word.

Determining an investment's level of risk

Type of Risk	Level of Risk		
	Low	Medium	High
Political risk			
Market risk			
Business risk			
Taxation risk			
Quality risk			
Volatility risk			
Technology risk			
Inflation risk			
Currency risk			
Interest rate risk			
Commodity risk			
Emotional risk			
Timing risk			
Information risk			
Liquidity risk			

Strategies to control risk

Risk Management and Strategy
Diversity by country. Underweight emerging markets.
Diversify by asset class.
Diversify by sector.
Defer tax or employ strategies that lower tax.
Focus on companies with low debt, good management and consistent savings.
Dollar cost average. Time.
Buy users of technology, not designers of it.
Buy hard assets. Buy bonds indexed to inflation and interest rates.
Diversify by currency. Avoid high debt economies. Buy global companies.
Go short-term with floating rate investments when rates rise.
Buy vertically integrated companies.
Asset allocation. Know your sleep point.
Dollar cost average.
Determine accuracy of source.
Stay away from investments that do not have active buyers and sellers.

Jimmy the Greek and grade six math

The great odds-maker Jimmy the Greek had a peculiar smile. Most people didn't understand his "look" which telegraphed gambling's winning side. Jimmy the Greek represented the house, which wins in the long-term. Jimmy didn't advise people to become bookies. Instead, he recommended bets that placed the potential gambler against the house or on the high risk side of the bet. This Greek knew he had a golden goose that he could financially milk for all it was worth.

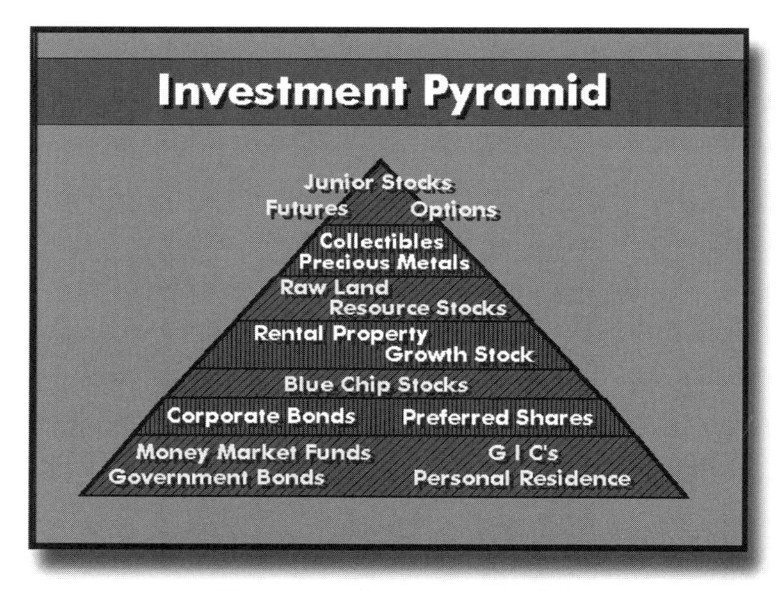

Know your investment's risk

The difference is in the odds

Most people know that gambling is a bet on an unlikely outcome. The rule of the gambling universe — the greater the risk of the unlikely outcome, the higher the expected payoff — attracts people to casinos, race tracks and bingos. Since betters rarely win, wealthy gamblers are the exception.

Investing is the opposite of high risk/high return behavior. This activity places your money into ventures where the odds are overwhelming in your favor. You should make an above-average return while taking modest risk. Since investing involves high probability behavior, not surprisingly, most wealthy people have become so because of their acute sense of knowing which bets have a high success ratio.

The statistical probability of investment choices

The previous risk/reward comments should be obvious to anyone with a grasp of grade six math. Yet, few people analyze an investment for its risk/reward relationship.

For example, if a breathless stock promoter tells you a company has a drug that is entering phase one of its clinical trials, hang up and don't buy the company's shares. Statistically, only one in 100,000 drugs that enter phase one clinical trials develop into commercial success.

The risks are phenomenal for start up diamond mines. Diamonds occur in a geological formations know as kimberlite pipes. To date, 50,000 kimberlite pipes have received serious drilling and exploration work. Of these 50,000, only 50 had enough mineralization to warrant mine development. With this investment, the odds of winning are about 1000:1, according to grade six math.

By putting money into things you understand, you can evaluate the risk. With inexperience you lose the ability to calculate the risks. When the odds are against you, you're gambling, not investing.

The arithmetic of loss

If you buy a stock that drops 50 percent, then your next investment has to double to get your capital back to ground zero. If the stock goes down by 80 percent, then your next choice has to rise by an incredible 400 percent to break even. It's almost impossible to recover from a big loss. Having the odds in your favor before you invest, ensures that you avoid this situation.

1 X 1 = bigger loser

One loser X another loser = an even bigger loser. Investors who continually ignore risk evaluation quickly find their chances of success drop geometrically, not arithmetically. Let's say a particular type of stock has a 1:10 probability of rising and making you money. If you buy two such stocks in a row, your chances of success have now dropped to 1:100 (10 x 10). If you buy three such stocks in a row, your chances are now 1:1000 (10 x 10 x 10). The moral: repeated high risk behavior becomes increasingly more devastating to your pocketbook the more you do it.

If you have a loss of...	You need a gain of...	If you have a gain of...	It takes a loss of...
-50%	100%	10%	-9%
-45%	82%	15%	-13%
-40%	67%	20%	-17%
-35%	54%	25%	-20%
-30%	43%	30%	-23%
-25%	33%	35%	-26%
-20%	25%	40%	-29%
-15%	18%	45%	-31%
-10%	11%	50%	-33%
-5%	5%	55%	-35%
... to breakeven		... to get back to even	

source: Dick Davis Digest

Jimmy's best tip
Jimmy the Greek made millions by betting when the odds were in his favor. If you are an investor, follow his example, but not his advice.

Storm proofing your investment portfolio

The current bull market is one of the biggest of all time. It will also be remembered as the one that nobody predicted. For years, financial experts said this market was extremely overvalued. As a result, it was long overdue for a cataclysmic drop of 1987 proportions. Regardless of the predictions, the market did the opposite as it bulldozed aside its detractors and powered from one new high to the next. Once again, it proved that trying to time markets is a mug's game.

However, these markets are trading at overvaluation levels that haven't been seen since early 1987. Years of continuously rising markets have not suspended the laws of economics. While overpriced markets never tell you exactly when they will crumble, they do indicate when you are closer to the end of the party than its beginning. Gravity will eventually pull this high flying market back to earth. When it happens, stock prices will drop dramatically.

Heed the storm warnings
High stock valuations place an individual's financial well-being at risk. Therefore, an investor should heed the current warning signs. Take steps to protect your stock portfolio from the damage that can be caused by a fierce bear (falling) market.

Sell your weak positions
Next, analyze each investment. Sell poor performers. If an investment can't rise in a strong market like this one, what will it do when markets turn sour?

Volatile stocks should be sold. These include equities in sectors like mining, forest products, technology and manufacturing. These groups tend to outperform their peers in bull markets and greatly underperform them in bad ones.

Raise cash levels
During periods of overvaluation, raising the cash level in a portfolio can increase liquidity and lower volatility. When you have more cash, you can buy stocks when they are undervalued. Secondly, short-term investments like treasury bills, money market funds and GICs are inherently stable by nature. They act like an anchor and lower the volatility of the entire portfolio when the going gets rough.

Sell the dogs
While it's never pleasant selling a losing stock position, doing so triggers a capital loss for tax purposes. These capital losses can be carried forward indefinitely, according to a 1997 Federal budget ruling. Losses can be applied against future capital gains incurred from selling profitable stocks. Every dollar of capital loss will neutralize the tax consequences of future capital gains.

Replace high volatile stocks
For non-market timers who prefer to remain fully invested, replace high risk equities with low risk ones. Industries like utilities, food processing, distilling and essential medical services produce products required in good and poor economic times. Since these companies maintain a steady earnings profile, they also have stable stock prices.

When storm clouds are on the horizon, the natural reaction is to seek refuge from the potential driving rain. In volatile markets, it makes sense to take the necessary precautions to protect a portfolio from the inevitability of falling stock prices. By seeking lower volatile investments and raising cash, you can minimize the damage of uneven markets.

Adding shock absorbers to your portfolio

Worrying or not worrying about an investment in a volatile market is a sign of its suitability. Sleepless nights, endless phone calls to your broker and staring at the stock ticker on the television or computer are signs that a portfolio is too aggressive.

A portfolio in keeping with an investor's risk tolerance needs little emotional maintenance. Surprisingly, many of the world's greatest and wealthiest investors treat their portfolio with selected neglect. Since they are confident in the inherent quality and balance of their investments, through good and bad times, they spend little time thinking about them. Confident, they leave their portfolio unmolested so it can achieve its long-term growth potential.

Richard Young, publisher of *Intelligence Report*, a successful investment letter, said he examined his portfolio for the first time last year in May. His investment statements were housed in a dust-covered folder. He stayed composed during 1998, a tough year — the highest level of stock market volatility in more than a decade.

A near-casual approach, like investment pro Richard Young, centers on asset mix. Don't put all your investment eggs into one basket. Unfortunately, many people dismiss this strategy because they believe a "sleep-well-at-night" portfolio is a dud. Research, however, shows that such a portfolio yields good performance and avoids sleepless nights.

Combine performance plus safety

A recent article in the *Wall Street Journal* demonstrated how different mixes of stocks and bonds fared between January 1945 and December 1997. A portfolio of 100 percent stocks provided a 12.9 percent annual compound return for the entire 52-year period. This portfolio had one bad year of -26.5 percent and eight separate years of losses greater than five percent. On the other hand, a portfolio consisting of 60 percent stocks and 40 percent bonds provided a solid 10.3 percent annual total return. This more conservative asset mix had a single worst year of -14.3 percent and only three years with losses greater than five percent.

This study has profound implications for the conservative investor who has a low tolerance for risk. It shows conclusively that an individual can achieve very acceptable rates of return while being exposed to modest levels of volatility. For most people, a 60/40 asset mix of stocks and bonds allows sufficient exposure to the stock market to generate reasonable returns. At the same time, it has a low risk bond category to avoid losses during market declines.

The stock market picture between 1926 and 1997 demonstrates the sensibility of a 60/40 asset mix. Over 71 years, the stock market (as measured by the S & P 500 index) declined on 20 annual occasions. In 18 of the 20 years, intermediate bonds (those with maturity between five and 10 years) rose. That is a 90 percent success ratio in portfolio defense. Moreover, in 1931 and 1969, when the intermediate bonds dropped, the losses were a minuscule 2.3 percent and .07 percent respectively. (Source: Richard C. Young's *Intelligence Report*, January 1999).

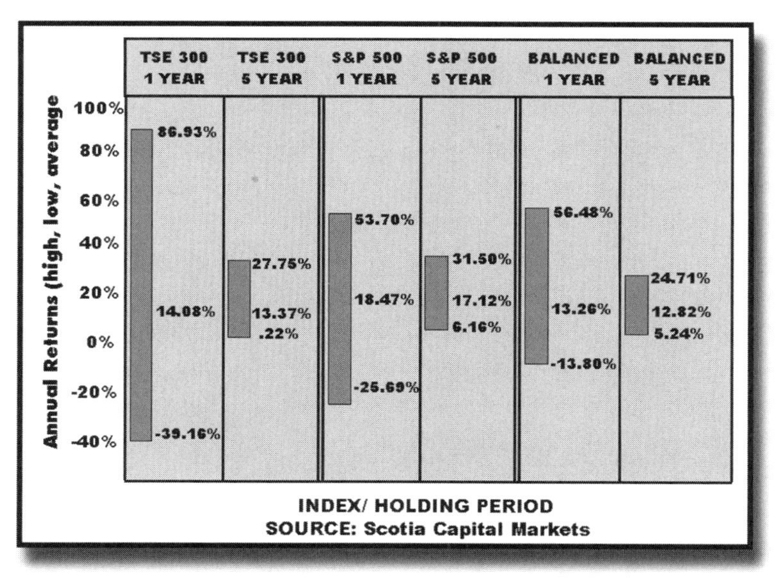

*** Balanced = 60% stocks/40% bonds**

Bonds are a shock absorber. Their price movement doesn't correlate with the stock market. Adding a percentage of bonds to a portfolio shields an investor from the stock market's punishment while still allowing it to benefit from its higher rates of return. A 60/40 portfolio is the best way to achieve reasonable returns without high anxiety.

CHAPTER 4

HOW TO KEEP FROM FINANCIALLY BLOWING YOUR BRAINS OUT

- A short course in human greed
- *The Wizard of Oz* and other scams
- Put your money where your mouth is
- Tune out market static
- Avoiding the most common investment errors
- Seven reasons why some people never make money

There are only two emotions on Wall Street:
fear and greed.

Anonymous

If all the financial experts in this country were laid
end to end, they'd still point in all directions.

Sam Ewing

Your emotions are often a reverse indicator of what
you ought to be doing.

John F. Hindelong

Don't try to buy at the bottom and sell at the top.
This can't be done, except by liars.

Bernard Beruch

A short course in human greed

The Bre-X mining fraud in Indonesia will probably be remembered as one of the greatest financial hoaxes of all time. The con was so well crafted that mining houses, stock exchanges, seasoned investors, and yes, even governments were completely taken by the ingenuity behind the sample tampering.

As incredulous as this story seems, it's just the latest in a long history of frauds and scams that have left a legacy of shearing untold numbers of financial sheep out of their life savings.

The original Ponzi scheme

In the early 1900s, Carlo Ponzi, an eager and hungry 17-year-old Italian immigrant, arrived in the US. After serving numerous prison terms for petty crimes, Ponzi implemented a scheme that launched him into the con artist big league.

In 1918, Ponzi opened Securities Exchange Company in downtown Boston. His business was simple — you give me some money and I'll give it back to you in 90 days, with 50 percent interest. Within two years the wildly successful Ponzi expanded to 35 branch offices to service his 40,000-plus investors.

Curious to know how his money machine could so effortlessly and risklessly spin out 50 percent profits every 90 days, the federal government investigated. Ponzi's elaborate "rob Peter to pay Paul" business plan was exposed. To pay investors back their 50 percent profits, Ponzi went to the next investor, made him the same deal and used the proceeds to pay back the first investor. This worked as long as the supply of new investors was larger than the supply of those being paid out.

Once the scam unravelled, the penniless Ponzi served five years for embezzlement. He soaked his trusting clients for more than $15 million. Poverty stricken, almost blind and partially paralyzed, Ponzi died in 1949 in a charity ward in Brazil.

A sucker is born every minute

In the mid-1980s, investors were hauled into a New York hotel to meet the world's most famous wheeler-dealer, the Saudi arms broker and crown prince of playboys, Adnam Khashoggi. The breathless prince gushed over the enormous amounts of gold, diamonds and precious metals in King Solomon's Mines, a mining concession in Mali, a west African country. A press release said the gold reserves were so large that they would "help stabilize world finances." Film legend Elizabeth Taylor, who "coincidently" dropped by the hotel, enthralled the audience.

None of the star struck investors asked how or why King Solomon's Mines ended up in Mali. Traditionally, the mines were thought to be in Zimbabwe, on the other side of the African continent.

Investors discovered that the emperor, or in this case the prince, wasn't wearing any clothes. The desperate Khashoggi manufactured a mining scam to save his US businesses from bankruptcy. Once again, scores of gullible investors lost their financial shorts.

Scams are inevitable

"Investing venture capital is a tricky business, but at least speculators should be able to lose their money honestly," one stockbroker recently said. Unfortunately, regardless of legislation or scrutiny, people will develop scams to prey upon the financially unwary. Human greed is impossible to control and even harder to legislate against. As long as there are people who dream of parlaying a small amount of money into a pot of gold with little regard for risk, there will continue to be an endless supply of the unscrupulous willing to take advantage of them.

The Wizard of Oz and other scams

A gold mine is a hole in the ground
with a liar on top.

Mark Twain

The Wizard of Oz gives us some fabulous insights behind a successful con artist. Here's a brief refresher of the story. Dorothy, a young Kansas farm girl, gets caught in a violent storm. A tornado deposits Dorothy and her house in the land of Oz. She begins her quest to get to the Emerald City, where a great wizard has the magical powers to help her get back to Kansas. On her journey, she meets a scatter-brained scarecrow, a cowardly lion, and a tin man without a heart. The quartet face many dangers and overcome insurmountable obstacles to reach the fabled city. In the throne room of the great wizard, Dorothy discovers he's really a little man behind a curtain controlling a slickly orchestrated pyrotechnic display. While this charlatan convinces everyone he's a wizard, Dorothy sees through his charade.

In the world of money, many financial wizards promise to make you rich. Here are seven rules which will help you separate the pretenders from the real players.

Rule 1 — If you can't dazzle them with brilliance, baffle them with BS

Good investments don't need to be sold, they sell themselves. Buyer beware, when substance is replaced by salesmanship. Glitz and glamour often cover the deficiencies of a poor investment.

Rule 2 — If it's too good to be true, then it's definitely too good to be true

Warren Buffet is probably the modern era's most successful investor. His portfolios have averaged over 30 percent per annum for decades. Buffet, who is worth at least $40 billion, says he has seen less than 20 good investments in his lifetime. Over age 60, this man has successfully spent a lifetime evaluating investments. If a slick promoter is continually presenting you with a once-in-a-lifetime opportunity, be cautious. If Warren Buffet has seen only 20 in his lifetime, your probability of repeatedly finding one is practically nonexistent.

Rule 3 — Do what I say, don't do what I do

Most people in the investment business have made their money by taking fees off other people, not by investing themselves. Before buying anything, find out if the salesperson is following his or her own advice or making money by having you follow it.

Rule 4 — In a lottery, only one in a million makes a million

Lotteries always focus on the one winner and avoid the 999,999 losers. Remember, investments with the potential to make you a lot of money are long shots. You probably know as many people who have gotten rich from a single investment as have won a lottery. This should tell you something.

Rule 5 — An elevator goes fast in both directions

The alarm bells should ring when someone tells you how much money you'll make on an investment. Higher returns are ALWAYS associated with higher risks. Put another way, the faster it goes up, the faster it can go down. Any investment that can double your money in a week can also cut it in half.

Rule 6 — Chicken Little says the sky is falling

Financial promoters use fear, one of the most powerful human emotions, to scare you into buying their book, taking their course, or purchasing their investments. Avoiding a huge financial catastrophe is their usual pitch. The promoter is supposed to hold the key to protecting your assets and making you prosper. Much of this advice involves buying gold (which is down by 65 percent over the last 20 years).

Rule 7 — Let's take your money and my experience and turn it into my money and your experience

A fast way to lose your capital is to rapidly trade your investments. This is especially true if you're involved in stocks and commodities where every transaction has a fee. Only about three percent of all traders ever make any money. Yet, the person who completes the transactions for you makes money, even if you don't.

The moral of *The Wizard of Oz* is that each character has to do his or her own work to make wishes come true. The cowardly lion performs a heroic act and becomes courageous. The tin man has compassion for a distressed soul and discovers he really has a heart. The scarecrow displays smart thinking and finds his brains. Dorothy clicks her red shoes and she and her dog, Toto, return to Kansas. Through hard work — not the wizard's magic — wishes become reality.

In real life, wealth is created by investing in quality and then holding for the long-term. Following this unmagical, realistic strategy will never turn you into a real wizard — just a financial one.

Put your money where your mouth is

A commitment of money is often the greatest diviner of intent. This is especially true in investing. In fact, most sophisticated money managers follow a basic principle: they won't invest in anything unless they see an equal commitment coming from the other side of the table. A plaque prominently displayed on a very successful venture capitalist's desk sums it up best, "Put your money where your mouth is. If you don't show me your money — I will never show you mine." Answer the following questions. If the answer is no, perhaps you should respond the same way to the investment you're considering.

1. Are company employees putting their money where their mouth is?

A company and its stock does better when employees have a significant financial stake in the ownership. A recent study by American Capital Strategies showed that between 1992 and 1997, companies with at least 10 percent employee ownership had a cumulative gain of 193 percent versus around 140 percent for the US stock market, as a whole.

Unfortunately, many companies have management or employee groups that don't see the advantage of making every staff member a direct participant in the financial future of the business.

2. Are the promoters putting their money where their mouth is?

Brokers, promoters and other salespeople earn a fee or commission only when he or she sells something. Remuneration is seldom tied to an investment's performance. With no link between his or her financial outcome and yours, you can only determine a marketer's level of conviction by his or her personal holding in the investment. Tread carefully and find out why if it's little or none.

3. Are the "insiders" putting their money where their mouth is?

The best predictor of a company's future performance is the trading activity of its officers, directors and major shareholders. They receive information about a company's future prospects long before the general public. When insiders are adding to their ownership of the company it's positive. When they're heading for the exits caution flags should wave.

It's almost impossible to obtain insider information on private companies. Public companies are a different story. By law, officers, directors and major shareholders of public companies must disclose their buying and selling activity to the stock exchange which lists the shares. A weekly, public report is issued.

For individual investors, the Canadian newsletter *Market Insider Bulletin* and the American newsletter *Insider's* present statistical data on insider trading in an understandable format. The financial insights you'll gain will more than cover the reasonable subscription cost.

Following the insider's leads — the smart money — is a profitable indicator on buying and selling stocks.

Ask the following question before buying any investment, "Are you willing to put your money where your mouth is?" If the answer is no, then don't show them any of your money until they are willing to show you theirs.

Tune out market static

It's frustrating having your favorite song drowned out by unwanted static. You immediately fiddle with the radio tuner, trying to find a stronger signal, without the popping and crackling. Like radio static, there's also market static. Stock market information is often accompanied by high levels of background noise, which can easily drown out the financial big picture.

Market noise is usually a flood of analysts who try to uncover the causal factors driving short-term stock market movement. This information is enormous during periods of high market volatility. Unfortunately, most of this analysis and prediction is about as useful as the static on the radio. Study after academic study shows that trying to predict the movement of interest rates, currencies, inflation, precious metals, economic growth, and stock markets is a waste of time. A monkey flipping a coin could be equally as successful. Heads or tails?

One such example is a recent research report completed by Dreman Value Management. Going back to 1982, the company cataloged yearly earnings estimates made by both economists and analysts for the 500 American companies comprising the S & P 500 index. Over the 15-year span covered by the research, analysts predicted that earnings would rise on average by 21.86 percent per year. As the numbers reveal, both groups of soothsayers were too optimistic. The average annual earnings growth projected by the analyst group was almost three times greater than the actual numbers over the 15-year period. Economists were slightly better, overestimating earnings growth by an annual average of 130 percent.

A less scientific but equally revealing activity is to peruse last year's economic predictions. Most of the crystal ball reading was so far off the mark it was embarrassing.

Prediction addiction leads to analysis paralysis

While the inconsistency of most financial analysis is almost comical, it affects the behavior of the typical investor. Deluged by an avalanche of inaccurate and often contradictory information, an individual can easily become confused and indecisive. Feeling overwhelmed, an investor may park investment money on the sidelines until the investment picture is clearer. Thus, the saying: investors caught up with prediction addiction suffer from analysis paralysis.

Tune out the noise

Look at the big picture. Tune out the static. A quality portfolio of diversified investments held over a long period and added to systematically, will eventually compound its way to substantial wealth. Regrettably, those who listen to the static never adopt this program. If they do, they can't stick with it long enough to make good things happen.

The following advice, written by an ordinary Joe with an average education and a very successful 20-year investment history, is a good strategy for tuning out market noise:

So keep your stock, I do advise,
The longer kept, the price will rise,
Buy low, keep long whene'er you can,
Ignore the Fed and Al Greenspan.

Isa Mushmawar
Time, December, 1997

Avoiding the most common investment errors

A savvy old investor once said that it's not what you do right that makes you rich, but rather, what you don't do wrong. According to him, if you lose 50 percent on an investment, then you have to double your money on the next one just to break even. He suggests there are two important rules of investing:

Rule 1 — Don't lose your principal
Rule 2 — Never, never, never forget Rule 1

It is more difficult to recover from a mistake, than not making it at all. While this is a negative view of investing, it will likely keep you out of the poor house. These are the 10 most common mistakes stock market investors make. Hopefully, these rules will keep you from wasting your money on unsuccessful strategies.

Mistake 1 — Investing without a strategy

Goals shape where you want to go and how you get to your destination. Without them, an investor will float from one stock to another and chase yesterday's overpriced flavor of the month. The person without the discipline to implement a long-term strategy is doomed to incur continual losses and rudderless performance.

You need knowledge to develop an investment strategy. Reading about the techniques and philosophies of successful investors like John Templeton, Warren Buffet and Peter Lynch can easily take five years off your learning curve.

Mistake 2 — Not measuring risk before reward

Reward is always secondary to risk. With investments such as options, futures and junior stocks, there is a five percent chance you'll win and a 95 percent chance you will lose. Investing is simply playing the odds. Unless you can purchase an investment with an 80 percent chance of winning, don't consider it for part of your core portfolio. Only buy a stock when the odds of winning are overwhelming in your favor.

Mistake 3 — Trading your way to financial oblivion

Your long-term performance is inversely proportional to your trading activity. Trading triggers taxes and transaction costs. This money goes into other people's pockets. Since it's impossible to repeatedly pick winners, most traders lose money. Most individuals who make money investing do so by buying quality and holding for the long-term.

Mistake 4 — Ignoring inflation and taxes

Many investors lose money because they don't consider the effects of inflation and taxes. Let's say your investments are growing at a rate of four percent per year in today's environment of 50 percent taxes and two percent inflation. The investment has a return of zero in real terms when these two negatives are included. The return after taxes and inflation is the measure of a portfolio's true performance.

Mistake 5 — Keeping your losers

In the children's story, Sarah Cynthia Stout would not take the garbage out. She'd scour the pots, scrape the pans, candy the yams and spice the hams. Although her daddy would scream and shout, she simply would not take the garbage out.

Don't let garbage build in your portfolio. Get rid of the losers. Sell the dogs! Reallocate your money toward investments with growth potential. Considering taxes, selling creates losses which can later be used to offset future gains and thus reduce or eliminate future tax on your profits.

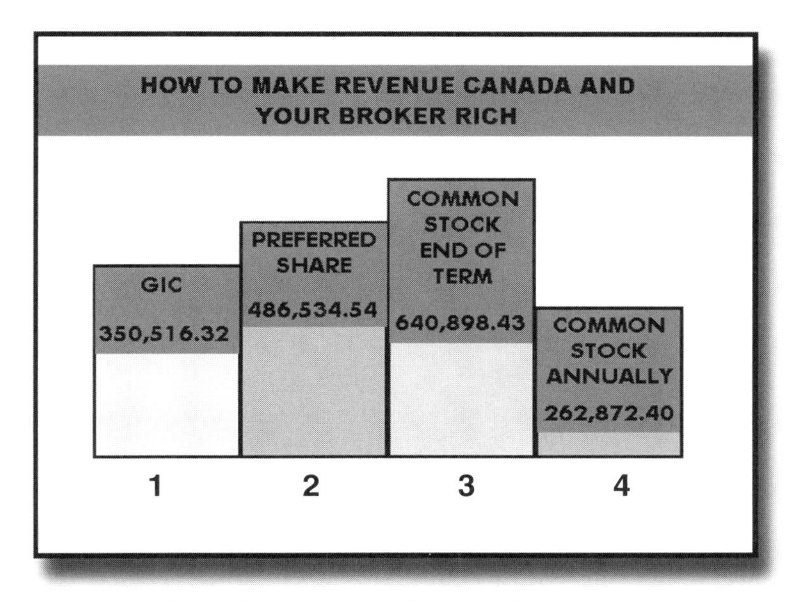

The graph shows the dramatic after tax difference over 20 years between buying $100,000 worth of GIC's, preferred shares and common stock. All investments are assumed to grow at 12 percent per year. Graph 3 assumes that a portfolio of stocks were bought and held for 20 years. Graph 4 assumes that the portfolio was turned over once a year for 20 years. Taxes were paid annually and a two percent brokerage firm commission was charged to buy and sell the securities.

Mistake 6 — Trying to time the market

Although economists, investment analysts and assorted financial gurus have much cerebral horsepower, their predictions are accurate less than 50 percent of the time. You could do equally as well by flipping a coin. Trying to time markets, interest rates, economic cycles and other such arcane pursuits is fruitless. Systematically buy high quality assets on a regular basis. Then hold them for the long-term. This method works better than any other investment program ever devised.

Mistake 7 — Ignoring dividends

Over many business cycles, common stocks have provided an average nine percent return. A full 50 percent of that return comes from the annual cash payouts or dividends. As these companies have become more profitable, they have increased the amount of that dividend by 4.5 percent per year. A company is a winner if it has a history of dividend increases. If the dividend is increasing, the price of the company's shares is likely increasing.

Mistake 8 — Ignoring widow and orphan stocks
When considering stocks, look for companies in industries with staying power. For example, are you planning to haul water from the nearest creek? Are you planning to read your book by flashlight? Perhaps you were thinking of heating your home by campfire this winter. Everyone uses water, electricity and natural gas. Make the blue chip companies in these industries a core part of your portfolio. These companies may be called widow and orphan stocks, but their performance has mirrored that of the market as a whole with much less risk.

Mistake 9 - Investing on emotion
No investment will make you rich overnight. Therefore, avoid the emotional whirlwind of believing you can find a "one-in-a-million" investment. That venture has 999,999 failures.

Mistake 10 — Starting too late
If Jane invests $1,200 every year between the ages of 25 and 32 and then doesn't invest again, she will have $227,000 by the age of 65, assuming a nine percent return. If Joe invests $1,200 per year starting at age 33 and invests the same amount at nine percent each year until the age of 65, he will have earned $215,000. Joe invests four times as much as Jane and has less to show. A little invested early beats much invested late. Compounding is the eighth wonder of the world.

While obvious, these mistakes prevent most people from profiting in the stock market. Unfortunately, most individuals spend about five years in the school of hard knocks learning that it's easier and less costly to avoid making the mistakes in the first place.

Seven reasons why some people never make money

The market, like the Lord, helps those
who help themselves.
But, unlike the Lord, the market does not forgive
those who know not what they do.
Warren Buffet

Over the last 20 years a $1,000 investment in the Canadian stock market would have grown into $8,279. This represents an annual growth rate of about 10.3 percent. Despite a total return of over 800 percent, many people have never made money investing in equities.

Fortunately, people's mistakes are easily corrected. Here are some of the factors that help to minimize your investment dollars.

Reason 1 — Insufficient firepower

Financial firepower means having enough cash on hand to meet all the requirements of day-to-day living, without having to cash in long-term investments prematurely for an emergency.

An example: your broker offers you an excellent stock that's fallen from $27 to $16. It's a good deal, because the company is expected to bounce back in the short to medium term. You scoop up every dime, every loonie, to buy a stock you know will let you retire 10 years ahead of schedule.

Two months later the orthodontist says your son's teeth will cost $3,000. You don't have the firepower to ride the stock's recovery to $25 in two year's time. You sell the stock, the most liquid asset you have for $13. Murphy's Law: the need to fix family teeth always occurs when your investments are at their lowest ebb.

Reason 2 — Mistaken identity

Fine tailored clothes, foreign cars, yachts, and backyard swimming pools have a common denominator. They exude the look of wealth. However, the look is costly. Most items that flaunt wealth are depreciating assets. In other words, over time, they go down in value. Real wealth is built by investing in stocks, bonds, real estate or a small business. These assets hold a promise of a return on investment. Over time, these investments produce profits so you'll look wealthy, and actually be wealthy.

Reason 3 — Lack of time

Serious money is made slowly over time. The chances of making a quick killing in the stock market are about the same as winning a lottery. Both have odds of over one million to one.

Most long shots have bigger risks than rewards. If it sounds too good to be true, it probably is.

Reason 4 — Fear

Fear creates and drives the herd mentality. When a stock is low, fear is the motivator. Fearing the stock will go lower, people frantically sell. The herd doesn't understand common sense. Buying more of a good stock, when it's at an ebb and bargain priced is a prudent idea.

Oil is a classic example of how fear paralyzes reason. When the crude was selling at record high levels of $40 US per barrel, brokerage firms were swamped with people trying to buy energy stocks. At $10 per barrel, nobody wanted to buy any.

The herd mentality has been evident since the Neanderthals. The intelligent loner, who exercises reason, ignores the stampede of panic, and is skeptical about the popular press and fearful friends, usually makes the bucks. Driven by fear and greed, a small investor misses the party. It's over when he or she arrives. Or he or she leaves before it begins.

Reason 5 — Greed

Why do sane, reasonable, middle-class people think it's possible to find an investment that will multiply 100 times within 10 minutes of making the investment? If someone tells you how much money you're going to make, they'll ALWAYS tell you about the positives. They'll NEVER explain the negatives.

Reason 6 — Under diversification

One argument says you should stick to investing in a small number of positions. This could be profitable if the economy and your investment is good. If the investment doesn't do well this could mean financial disaster.

A more compelling argument suggests you ought to diversify. By spreading your investments you won't be knocked out by one company's failure, a slump in one sector of the economy or a recession in one region of the country.

Chance favors the mind that is prepared, said Louis Pasteur. Learning how to make money and keep it are important money management principles.

Reason 7 — Impatience

At a return of 10 percent, money doubles in seven years, quadruples in 14 years and increases by a multiple of 16 times in 28 years. For the average individual, this means the key to wealth building is letting time and compound interest work its magic.

Given enough time and patience, even ordinary investments like bonds and GICs can produce an exceptional return. When your motives are not fear, greed or impatience, you'll gain in the long run. Serious money is made slowly over time.

CHAPTER 5

PLANNING FOR RETIREMENT

- Preparing for a career change: from wage earner to investment manager
- Will you have enough money to retire?
- Making early retirement happen
- Learning important lessons from the Chicken Little School of Financial Planning
- RRSP strategies for busy people
- The answers to the most commonly asked RRSP questions

Financial success is never having to balance your checkbook.

Benjamin Graham

To turn $100 into $110 is work. To turn $100 million into $110 million is inevitable.

Edgar Bronfman

Preparing for a career change: from wage earner to investment manager

People who are currently making the change from wage earner to retirement are among Canada's thriftiest generations. Many have saved between 10 and 15 percent of their annual income. Over a 30 to 40-year working life, this translates into $250,000 or more in assets.

There is, however, a big difference between knowing how to earn this money and knowing how to invest it. We spend one-third of our lifetime learning, one-third of our lifetime earning and one-third of our lifetime in retirement. We receive much training in earning, but one has to actively pursue training in investing.

Getting an investment education

Preparing for a career is one of the central focuses of our lives. We start in kindergarten at the age of five. For some, the journey doesn't end until his or her late 20s after eight years of university.

This effort is considered the price of survival in our knowledge-intensive world. To make a dime, you have to put in the time. In fact, with knowledge doubling every five years, the current workplace demands continual upgrading to keep from becoming a dinosaur.

Like any new career, your investment education needs a commitment of time and energy. The financial community suggests this is a difficult task. However, getting a financial education is easier than you might think.

Initially, when I interviewed over 1,000 financially successfully individuals I expected superior intelligence to be a commonality among these people. To my surprise, I.Q. was not a prevalent factor. In fact, most of the basic investment principles require common sense, not a Ph.D. in finance.

My research also revealed a surprising fact concerning the time spent studying the financial markets and overseeing a portfolio. On average, a financially successful person spent only two hours each week managing his or her money. If we can spend 40 hours per week earning it, then a couple of hours per week on management shouldn't be a big burden.

Financial tools can work for you

There are basic financial tools that are effective in protecting your money and helping it grow during retirement. Understanding what they are and how they work is essential. A good place to get these financial tools, and one of the best starting points on your financial education is an investment class offered through a community college. This will give you a good overview of the subject and steer you toward important information. Much of today's financial literature is either impossible to understand or totally impractical in the real world.

A subscription to a daily newspaper like the *Globe and Mail* or the *National Post* will provide you with current and timely information.

Find someone — a mentor — who understands investing, is an unbiased source of advice, and is a sounding board for your ideas.

Start your financial education early. The more time you spend preparing for a career in managing your money, the more likely you are to be a success.

A good financial education must also teach you how to maximize change. In the early 1980s, taxes were lower, oil was $40 per barrel, gold was $800 per ounce, interest rates were 22 percent, inflation was at 16 percent and we had a 90-cent Canadian dollar. Today, we have higher taxes, oil is $20 per barrel, gold is $250 per ounce, interest rates are four percent, inflation is two percent and our loonie is about 70 cents against the US dollar. By any standard, this transition has been momentous. Yet, it probably won't be any less than our current decade.

Moving from earner to investor

Getting an investment education is critical to a financially successful retirement. We expend enormous effort as a wage earner. Sometimes, this effort overshadows the preparation needed for retirement.

During the transition to retirement we move from being an earner of money to being an investor of money. A good investment education will make the transition easier.

The importance of sound investing skills at this stage of life cannot be underestimated. Actuary tables indicate that the average life expectancy for men is 82 years and 87 for women. A woman who retires at 55 years of age could live another 32 years. This means her financial resources in retirement must last 32 years.

Since there is usually enough time to recover from all but the most serious errors, a younger person can afford to make financial mistakes. Mature adults don't have the same luxury. Recovery from major blunders is difficult because the individual doesn't have the same opportunities to go back into the work force to recoup the losses.

Since the ability to recover from financial mistakes is very limited at retirement, this isn't the time of life to be practicing with your money. Reducing spending is the only way to cope with a loss at this later stage in life. It might mean cutting out the extras like a golf club membership or an annual cruise. At the worst, it could result in the deprivation of the basics of food, clothing or even medical treatment.

Your level of skill as an investment manager, to a large degree, determines your lifestyle in retirement. Take the time and energy to successfully prepare for this stage of life. In many ways, retirement is the most important career change you'll ever make.

Will you have enough money to retire?

Will your current savings and investment program be sufficient to provide for your needs at retirement? By analyzing your needs in retirement and preparing a budget you can know for sure.

How much will retirement cost?

Any foray into retirement planning starts with an appraisal of your income needs at retirement. A good rule of thumb is that most people can comfortably maintain their existing lifestyle on 60 percent of their pre-retirement income. However, if you plan to move to an area where expenses are higher or your retirement includes expensive travel or hobbies, your retirement income may need to be equal or greater than your pre-retirement income.

The only way to attach a cost to your retirement is to determine the type of lifestyle you want. After you've established your retirement lifestyle, then you can translate this into dollars and cents by preparing a simple budget.

Estimating income sources at retirement

The next step in the financial planning process is to estimate sources of income. Retirement income is derived from three main sources: government benefits, company pension plans and personal savings.

Consider government retirement benefits

Old Age Security (OAS) is paid to Canadian residents over the age of 65. Even if you have never worked outside the home, you are eligible for benefits. If you have a high income, then your OAS income will be adjusted downward. The maximum OAS benefit is approximately $400 per month. A guaranteed income supplement of up to $490 per month is also available if certain conditions are met.

If you have been steadily employed over your working life, you've likely made the maximum contributions and will be eligible for Canada Pension Plan (CPP) benefits of approximately $750 per month. If you have been contributing less than the maximum, or haven't been working steadily, your benefits will be reduced. While you can receive your benefits anytime between 60 and 70 years of age, the sooner you take your pension the less you get.

For the latest figures on both the Canada Pension Plan and Old Age Security, contact Health and Welfare Canada listed in the blue pages of your telephone book.

Review your company pension plan

The majority of employers (approximately 61 percent) don't offer any form of a pension plan. If you're part of the lucky minority with a plan, you may be entitled to payments from a Registered Pension Plan or Deferred Profit Sharing Plan.

Some company plans guarantee a pension income based on your salary and years of service with the company. With this plan, your employer should accurately be able to tell you how much your pension will pay you upon retirement.

With another company pension plan, the benefit at retirement is based on how well your funds do over the period they are invested. With this type of plan, your employer can only roughly estimate your retirement benefits.

Determine your personal savings

Calculating the worth of your personal savings at retirement is simple. First, add up the total amount of money that you have invested or have available to invest now. Next, determine your future investments on a monthly or yearly basis. Finally, multiply these figures by the number of years that you have left until retirement and by the expected rate of return.

At this point, a good investment (for as little as $30) is a calculator that computes compound interest. It takes about half an hour to learn how to use this calculator, after which you can easily crunch through a compound interest calculation in about 15 seconds.

When making these calculations, consider two cautionary notes. First, don't overestimate your rate of return. Over 30 years, stocks have averaged an annual return of about 10 percent per year and bonds about nine percent per year. Secondly, don't underestimate inflation's power on eroding the value of your money. When calculating the rate of return on your investments, subtract the rate of inflation from the investment to get your real rate of return after inflation.

Put it all together

After adding up all your sources of income and comparing them with your expenses at retirement, ideally your income exceeds your needs. If it doesn't, you have four choices:

First, decrease your lifestyle (i.e. cut your future standard of living) at retirement;

Second, increase your savings rate (i.e. reduce your present standard of living);

Third, try and increase the rate of return on your investments (i.e. take on more risks);

Fourth, keep working extra years until you have enough money to retire (i.e. postpone retirement).

Do it now

A financial plan, like the one outlined above, can easily be completed in an afternoon. In a few hours you can create a financial road map that will lead to a comfortable, worry free, and financially secure retirement.

Making early retirement happen

If we are to believe the advice given by some of our profoundest financial thinkers, the average Canadian needs at least $1 million on gold watch day or he or she will outlive his or her money. However, with a thimble-full of common sense, and a little moxie, you could retire much sooner with much less.

In reality, most Canadians can and do retire with incomes between $30,000 and $40,000 per year. They still eat out, travel, golf, and enjoy a comfortable lifestyle. While they have to watch their pennies, they don't live like hermits. Here are some suggestions on how to make early retirement happen.

Downsize

Many people are asset rich and cash poor at retirement. However, this can usually be solved by selling off extras like vehicles, raw land, businesses, farms, recreational toys or unneeded furnishings. Downsizing to a smaller home is also a good strategy. Less square footage means less time devoted to maintenance. Taxes and utility costs are lower. The money saved from buying a smaller and cheaper house, combined with the cash from asset liquidation can be substantial. If this available cash is invested in securities that produce income, it's often enough to swing the balance in favor of early retirement.

Don't completely retire

A huge hole often remains when people retire. Work provided numerous benefits, besides finances. A challenge in retirement is filling your time with meaningful activities. For many people, the idea of semi-retirement makes smart emotional and financial sense.

For the self-employed, a partner can participate in running the business. This can allow for more leisure time while still providing an income stream. Other individuals might want to pursue part-time work or start a small business.

By working part-time you can retire many years earlier than planned. Those who need extra stimulation also have a vehicle through which they gradually ease into their golden years.

Don't move to Lotus Land

Retiring to British Columbia seems to be every Albertan's dream. Yet, those who move often get a huge shock. In B.C., income taxes are 20 percent higher, houses are double the price, provincial sales tax is added to GST, and the cost of basic items is outrageous.

For a sensible compromise, keep your principal residence in Alberta (one of the least expensive areas in North America to live). Then use some of the money you've saved to finance a trip down south every winter (or to Lotus Land).

Use your principal

Most retirement calculations are based on living on a portfolio's income without touching the principal. However, unless you are planning to leave a big legacy to charity or relatives, start dipping into the investment principal as you get older. Reworking calculations to include the spending of principal can shave years off retirement date projections.

How to maintain a lifestyle at half the cost

Routine maintenance on the house and car, cooking more meals at home and having a garden saves money. You can save from 50 to 90 percent of the cost of goods by buying from auctions, discount travel shops, garage sales, flea markets and through classified advertising. By going to the discount night at the movies, using two for one coupons, and playing on public instead of private golf courses, you can live like a king on a pauper's budget.

Why wait?

You can't make more time. There is some truth to this saying. However, with early retirement you can cheat. While you can't make more of it, with proper planning, you can make the most of it.

Learning important lessons from the Chicken Little School of Financial Planning

In the fairy tale, Chicken Little gets hit on the head with an acorn. Then she scares her barnyard friends into believing that the sky is falling in. The financial industry must believe Ms. Little. They too, are resorting to the odious tactic of fear mongering.

Through a rather brilliant combination of statistical misinformation and convoluted logic, these "supposed gurus" are scaring people into believing distortions. According to them, unless you can stash millions of dollars prior to retirement, your golden years will be very tarnished. You'll sleep on a park bench and only be able to afford to eat cat food (and not even the fancy variety).

Now fear mongering isn't necessarily a bad idea, when you consider that the average Canadian spends 86 percent of his or her take-home pay on debt service. However, frightening people into believing they need unrealistically high levels of wealth to retire often has the opposite effect. With the mark so unattainable, and feeling hopeless in the pursuit, people are dissuaded from even marginally saving. After all, why accumulate assets for the future if an average person can't even come close to the lofty targets for a minimum comfortable retirement proposed by financial experts? If the future is going to be bleak, why not live for today, and enjoy the present?

To come up with a workable retirement plan, it's important to have a clear view of the variables that will affect your future cash flow. To do that, let's destroy some popular myths.

Myth 1 — The Canada Pension Plan (CPP) is bankrupt

Obviously, if nothing is done over the next 20 years, the doomsayers will be right about the future of the Canada Pension Plan. Recent working papers on how to fix the CPP suggest some innovative solutions to ensure its long-term sustainability. These include raising premiums, gradually raising the age of eligibility to 67 and even privatizing the system to make it self-funding like Singapore's successful plan. Currently, CPP's maximum benefit is $751 per month. For a husband and wife qualifying for the maximum, this is a comfortable income of $1,502 per month.

Myth 2 — Inflation will eventually reduce your retirement nest egg to nothing

Over the past 50 years the average inflation rate has been four percent. However, inflation tends not to affect retired people as much as younger people. Many retirees own their own homes, replace automobiles infrequently, spend less on clothing, have few work-related expenses and have already furnished, housed and fed their families. Due to reduced spending, the inflationary effects on the average retired couple are about half of those of a younger couple with a growing family. For example, a 2.5 percent inflation rate reduces buying power by 50 percent every 29 years, whereas an inflation rate of five percent minimizes buying power by half every 14 years. The inflation factor used in your retirement planning greatly affects your retirement income.

Myth 3 — You plan to make your relatives rich

You will need much more money if you plan to leave most of your principal to your kids or a charity. Using some of the principal to supplement your income makes life more comfortable. Most financial planners base their calculations on leaving your principal intact.

Reality check

Couples retiring with maximum CPP benefits can comfortably live on savings of $200,000 to $300,000. This allows for winters in

Arizona, golf and dining out a few times a week. While everyone has different financial expectations, this should provide sufficient income for a comfortable retirement lifestyle. Plus, it's more realistic than following a panicked bird.

RRSP strategies for busy people

"The only RRSP strategy I have is to get the contribution into my RRSP account before the March 1 deadline."

Everyday pressures often leave little time for effective investment planning. For those of you who were born 15 minutes late and have never caught up, here are some ideas to make the most of your RRSP contribution.

Contribute your maximum
For 1999 contributions, you may contribute the lesser of $13,500 or 18 percent of your 1998 earned income. However, if you're a member of a Deferred Profit Sharing Plan or company pension plan, don't forget to subtract your pension adjustment from the

Rate of RRSP Growth at Different Contribution Levels
(10% annual rate of return)

	Annual Contribution			
	$,3000	$5,000	$10,000	$14,500
Value of the RRSP				
Year 1	$ 3,300	$ 5,500	$ 11,000	$ 15,950
Year 5	20,150	33,580	67,160	97,376
Year 10	52,590	87,660	175,310	254,202
Year 15	104,850	174,750	349,500	506,771
Year 20	189,010	315,010	630,020	913,536
Year 25	324,550	540,910	1,081,820	1,568,636

above calculated contribution figure. Your pension adjustment amount is located on the T-4 supplementary, filed with your 1998 income tax. If you need help, check your phone book for Revenue Canada's automated call-in service which tells you your personal RRSP contribution limit.

What to do if you're short on cash

If you're short on greenbacks, consider borrowing funds to make your contribution. Although the interest on borrowed money isn't a tax write-off, you can deduct your contribution which will then start growing tax free inside the RRSP. These two factors more than compensate for the interest you pay on the loan.

If you have a self-directed RRSP, consider making a contribution-in-kind, a non-cash equivalent. For example, put $5,000 in Canada Savings Bonds into your RRSP and you'll receive a full $5,000 credit. You can make a contribution-in-kind with any asset qualifying for an RRSP.

Look at spousal contributions

If either you or your spouse will be the major income earner at retirement, then consider making contributions to the lower income earner's RRSP. When taking money out of the RRSPs, the taxation will be more even between the two of you. The tax paid to Revenue Canada will also be lower.

Make your contribution early

The sooner you get your money into an RRSP each year, the longer it has to work for you without the effects of taxation. If you contributed $13,500 at the beginning of the year for the next 25 years at a 10 percent rate of return, you would amass $1,460,454. Made at the end of the year the same RRSP would become $1,327,685 or $132,769 less.

Check for missed contributions

Since 1991 you can carry forward unused RRSP contributions. Any missed contribution since 1991 can be added to this year's contribution. As well, if you don't have enough money to make this year's contribution, it can be saved and used in future years when you have more resources.

Take advantage of increased foreign content limits

Up to 20 percent of the value of your RRSP can be invested in foreign securities. You can diversify out of the Canadian market and into faster growing areas of the world.

Over-contribute
You are allowed to make a lifetime over-contribution of $2,000 into an RRSP. Once inside the RRSP your money grows unmolested by tax until withdrawn. Before retirement, you'll want to use up this $2,000 as a contribution to avoid double taxation.

The answers to the most commonly asked RRSP questions

Contribution limits? Foreign content? How long can I contribute? What's not allowed in a plan? These and many other questions often arise concerning RRSPs. Like other investments, the rules constantly change. Here are some quick answers to the most commonly asked questions about RRSP rules.

Q: What are the RRSP contribution limits for 1999?
A: Your RRSP contribution limit for 1999 can be calculated as follows: You may contribute the lesser of $13,500 or 18 percent of your 1998 earned income plus any unused contribution room from previous years. If you're a member of a Registered Pension Plan or a Deferred Profit Sharing Plan, you must subtract your pension adjustment and/or past service pension adjustment (see your 1998, T-4 supplementary form which you filed with your taxes).

The maximum amount you can contribute to your RRSP in 1999 is determined by your income in 1998. Check your 1998 tax assessment, which lists your 1998 RRSP contribution amount plus any amount that you've carried forward from previous years.

Q: How much foreign content am I allowed in my RRSP?
A: Canadians are allowed to invest up to 20 percent of the purchase value of their RRSPs in foreign securities. This should be viewed as a serious investment option, as the global marketplace has historically outperformed the Canadian market.

Q: What happens if I can't contribute the maximum allowable to my RRSP?
A: You can take advantage of the carry forward provisions that came into effect in 1991. According to the 1996 Federal budget, you are now allowed to carry forward unused RRSP contribution room indefinitely.

Q: Are RRSP administration fees tax deductible?
A: No

Q: How much can I overcontribute to my RRSP?
A: You can overcontribute as much as $2,000 to your RRSP.

Q: What happens if my overcontribution exceeds $2,000 from previous years?
A: You have to use up the overcontribution and get it below $2,000 before you are allowed to make any additional RRSP contributions.

Q: What is the first day I can make my 2000 contribution?
A: January 2, 2000.

Q: What is the maximum I can contribute for 2000?
A: Maximum RRSP contribution limits for 1999 are $13,500. They're scheduled to remain at this level until 2004.

Q: Are there any investments that cannot be held in an RRSP?
A: Investments that don't qualify include: gold and silver bars; other precious metals; personal property such as art, antiques and gems; commodities and futures contracts.

Q: When do I have to collapse my RRSP?
A: The new rules state that an RRSP has to be collapsed or converted into an annuity or RIF by December 31 of the year you turn 69 years of age.

Q: Can I make non-cash contributions to my RRSP?
A: With a self-directed RRSP, you can make non-cash contributions. If you own an investment that qualifies for an RRSP, you can deposit it into your RRSP instead of cash. The deduction available for income tax purposes is determined by the market value of the security on the day of the deposit.

Q: Can I borrow from an RRSP to buy a house?
A: Yes, and there are two ways to do so. First, you can borrow money from your RRSP to purchase or refinance a house and then make monthly mortgage payments back to the RRSP until the debt is repaid.

Secondly, under the first-time home buyer's plan, you can borrow up to $20,000 from your RRSP as an interest free loan. The loan, however, must be paid back to the RRSP with a minimum of 15 equal installments over 15 years.

Q: How long does a spousal RRSP contribution have to stay in the RRSP before any withdrawals are taxed in the hands of the non-contributing spouse?
A: Three calendar years.

Q: Can children under 18 contribute to an RRSP?
A: Yes, as long as they have earned income.

Since RRSP rules are complex, check with your professional advisor on your particular situation.

CHAPTER 6

INCREASING YOUR INVESTMENT I.Q.

- Financial brain food
- Understanding stock market lingo
- Have fun making money — join an investment club
- Rx for information overload
- Classic investment advice from Fisher and Graham
- Understanding bull and bear markets

A bull market tends to bail you out of all your mistakes. Conversely, bear markets make you pay for your mistakes.

Richard Russell

Financial genius is a rising stock market.

John Kenneth Galbraith

With enough inside information and $1 million you can go broke in a year.

Warren Buffet

In a rising market, the tendency to look beyond the simple fact of increasing value to the reasons on which it depends greatly diminishes.

John Kenneth Galbraith

Financial brain food

You need good, clear-headed advice and information to make it through today's financial maze. Here are my suggestions for some of the best written books on investment, finance and taxation.

Against the Gods: The Remarkable Story of Risk
by Peter Bernstein (John Wiley & Sons)

Understanding and managing risk is probably the most important skill an investor needs. For the more academic at heart, this book gives a history of the development of risk management.

The Millionaire Next Door
by Thomas Stanley and William Danko (Longstreet Press)

Most people have it all wrong when it comes to knowing how wealthy people got that way. It's rarely inheritance, advanced degrees or intelligence that builds fortunes. Wealth creation is the product of hard work, diligent savings, and living below your means. This books tells you about the seven common denominators of the wealthy.

The Warren Buffett Way
by Robert Hagstrom Jr. (John Wiley & Sons)

This book provides an in-depth look at the remarkable investment success of Warren Buffett who turned an initial investment of $100 into a $30 billion business empire. Hagstrom gives readers a plain-English analysis of the strategies and theories that have made Buffett the world's most prominent and successful investor.

The Vest Pocket Guide to Value Investing
by C. Thomas Howard (Dearborn Financial Publishing)

Howard translates the latest academic research about value investing into an easy-to-follow and clearly written guide. The average investor will benefit from Howard's academically tested strategies which provide superior performance over the longer term.

The Canadian Snowbird Guide
by Douglas Gray (McGraw-Hill Ryerson)

If you're one of the estimated one million Canadians who flee south every winter, this book is a must. It teaches you everything you need to know about living part-time in the United States, Mexico and Costa Rica.

What Works on Wall Street
by James P. O'Shaughnessy (McGraw-Hill)

This book should become the stock market classic of the 1990s. O'Shaughnessy has taken all the notable stock market strategies and has backtested them using 34 years of data to discover what really works on Wall Street.

Extraordinary Popular Delusions and the Madness of Crowds
by Charles Mackay (John Wiley & Sons)

While this book was written two centuries ago, it's a must read for anyone seeking a greater understanding of the stock market's frequently erratic behavior. Mackay explores the peculiar relationships between crowd psychology and market movement. His powerful advice contrasts most of today's fuzzy headed investment thinking. The book is more timely than it's ever been.

The Financial Post Smart Funds
by Jonathan Chevreau (Key Porter Books)

These yearly editions help investors make the best choices from more than 1,300 mutual funds on the market. It starts with a straightforward, five-step approach to choosing two or three core families. Then Chevreau identifies his 125 best buys.

KPMG Tax Planning for You and Your Family 1997
(Carswell Thompson Professional Publishing)

Taxation is an unruly beast. Fortunately, the specialists at KPMG do an excellent job of translating a very complex subject into practical techniques that will keep more hard earned dollars in your pocket and put fewer in Revenue Canada's.

Understanding stock market lingo

After talking to your stockbroker, you might feel like an explorer finding a lost tribe in the jungle — the experience is thrilling but the conversation clueless. To understand your broker's "Greek" here's a list of the most common financial lingo that he or she uses. The translation converts those buzzwords into plain-English.

ADR. An abbreviation for American Depository Receipt. Refers to some foreign shares trading on a US stock exchange.
Ask. The price at which an investor is willing to sell a particular stock or bond.
Asset allocation. The percentage of one's portfolio invested in a particular type of asset.
Average down. To buy more of an investment after it's dropped in price in an effort to lower the average cost.
Average up. To buy more of an investment after it's risen in price in an effort to capture more gain.
Bear market. A market where stock prices are falling.
Bid. The price at which an investor is willing to buy a particular stock or bond.
Blue chip. A term describing a large, high quality company.
Bull market. A market where stock prices are rising.
Convertible. Bonds or preferreds that are exchangeable for common shares.
Correction. Refers to a stock or a market that's going down.
Hold. The level at which an investment is neither cheap enough to buy nor expensive enough to sell.
Institution. Usually refers to a buyer or seller of investments such as a pension fund, mutual fund or other large professional manager of money.
I.P.O. This is an abbreviation for initial public offering. It refers to the first investment offering that a company makes to the buying public.
Junior. A term for a small start up company.
Large cap. A company where the total dollar value of its shares is among the very largest.
Margin. The amount a company is willing to lend you against securities held as collateral.

Margin call. When the value of securities held as collateral against a loan drops below a fixed level, the borrower is required to come up with additional capital to cover the shortfall or risk having the securities covering the loan sold.
Mid-cap. A company where the total dollar value of its shares is mid-sized compared to others.
Over bought. A market where excessive buying has pushed prices too high.
Over sold. A market where excessive selling has pushed prices too low.
Overweight. To raise the percentage of one's portfolio exposed to a particular type of investment.
P.E. An abbreviation for price earnings ratio. This is calculated by dividing a company's earnings per share by its stock price.
Preferred. Shares that rank above common stock in their claim to the company's assets.
Rally. Refers to a stock or market that is going up.
Rebalance. To change the asset mix of a portfolio.
Resistance. The top level of a price range that a stock or market will probably not rise above.
Small cap. A company where the dollar value of all its shares is very small.
Spread. The difference in price between what a buyer is willing to pay and a seller is willing to receive for a specific investment.
Stop loss. An order to sell an investment if it drops below a predetermined price.
Support. The bottom level of a price range that a stock or market will probably not go below.
Underweight. To lower the percentage of one's portfolio exposed to a particular type of investment.

Keep the list by the telephone. It will make the next conversation with your financial guru not only exciting but meaningful.

Have fun making money — join an investment club

Investment clubs are a good way for individuals to get started investing in the stock market and learn about the financial world. An investment club pools money, makes joint investments, offers an opportunity to learn about investing in a group setting and reduces the risk of going it alone. Even better, you'll likely make money at this hobby.

An investment club can have any number of investors placing money in different types of investments. It can also be as formal or informal as members desire. While clubs can meet as often as they like, most choose to meet monthly, with contributions made at every meeting. The performance of the club's portfolio is reviewed and new investments are discussed at each meeting.

There are a variety of clubs

To start a club, decide on your membership. Some clubs are large and actively recruit new members, while smaller clubs may be limited to friends or business associates. Larger clubs raise more money for investment. However, with the decision making process more difficult, individual members may not be as involved in the research of various investments.

When setting up your club, agree on a mutual investment philosophy. While most clubs invest in stocks, any kind of investment, from real estate to new business ventures, can be considered.

Like an individual investor, determine your investment objectives. Do you want to generate income, build equity or protect capital? It's important that all members agree on objectives.

Also consider the group's tolerance to risk. Whether conservative or risk-taking, your investment objectives and strategies should reflect the nature of your group. You may also want to consult a financial advisor who can assist you in selecting a range of investment vehicles.

Who decides?

Also consider how you'll make investment decisions. Many clubs select a group or an individual to research an investment. The research is presented to the group and membership votes on whether to proceed.

In a large club, a committee may research, make investment decisions, report actions and evaluate performance. It's a good idea to choose one person to make the trades with your broker.

Also determine where you'll get the money to invest. Generally speaking, the founding members contribute an amount to start the club. Thereafter, monthly contributions (or more frequently if desired) are made. Probably the best way to set up your club's finances is to have members buy units with their contribution. The value of these units fluctuates with the number of units outstanding and the value of the investments. This way, it's easier for existing members to leave (the club buys back their units) or for new members to join.

Voting procedures should also be determined. Members could be assigned one vote for each unit they own. Another option is to have each member assigned one vote regardless of the number of units they own.

A constitution is essential

A written statement of investment goals, risk tolerance, types of investments, voting and the decision making process (and other important information) should be in the club's constitution. This safeguards your club so established policies cannot be changed without the general agreement of a majority of members. This constitution, or charter, signed by each member is considered a legal contract. A lawyer can assist you in drawing up your charter. You can obtain sample charters from the Canadian Association of Investment Clubs or the Canadian Shareowners Association.

Investment clubs are a fun way to learn about investing. In addition, since you're probably pooling your funds with other members, you can purchase investments that may be too pricy on your own. Because you're investing money on a regular basis, it wll also help you to smooth out the market's volatility. This strategy, called dollar cost averaging, generally results in higher returns over time, rather than money invested all at once.

Are you bored with your current hobbies? Why not get some buddies together and start an investment club? The financial world is endlessly challenging. Plus, tightwads will enjoy making money, rather than spending it.

Rx for information overload

Many of us grew up in an era when we had to do everything ourselves. Previously, society rewarded those who could master many different skills. Back then, if you couldn't do a job yourself, it usually wouldn't get done.

Today's world is dramatically different, largely due to the onslaught of information. Prior to 1500 AD, knowledge doubled once every 1,000 years. The Renaissance in Europe and the invention of the printing press changed the world forever.

A cultural environment encouraged the discovery of knowledge. Technology produced and circulated this new information.

Between 1700 and 1900, knowledge doubled. Over the next 50 years it doubled again. Today, knowledge doubles every two years. By the early 2000s, knowledge will double every six months.

As knowledge rapidly accumulates, it's difficult to absorb and make sense of competing and conflicting information. Experts are needed to handle this explosion. Previously, we used experts as a source of information. With Internet access, 100-channel television and the explosion of print media, the equation is different. Professionals are needed to screen out the superfluous and direct us to the important. Today's experts are information sifters and sorters.

When applied to personal finance, information overload is chronic. The volume of information on products, services and strategies is overwhelming. When this information seems contradictory you can feel bewildered. Here are some suggestions on handling information overload.

Find hands that help — not pick your pocket

An average individual will occasionally need assistance to sort through the hurricane of information. A financial planner can help. These professionals will give you a financial road map, review your current financial position, establish your future goals and objectives, and then develop a realistic financial strategy for you. A financial planner can also explain the most appropriate investments to enable you to meet those goals "sans" the usual salesperson hype.

There are two types of financial planners. The first is called fee-for-service. These people charge a fee for preparing a financial plan, about $300, depending on how complicated your finances. As fee-for-service planners are not connected to any specific financial institution, they will generally give you a bias-free financial plan.

The second type of financial planner is like a mutual fund salesperson, stockbroker, insurance specialist or banker. They sell products for a specific company or group of companies. While they are qualified to draft a financial plan, it may be biased towards the products they sell. However, with this kind of planner, there is usually no charge for their advice. They make money by selling you investments. Since they handle the planning and investment side of the equation, you don't have to start fresh with another person when it's time to purchase the specific investments for your plan.

Financial planners have two recognized designations: Canadian Financial Planner (CFP); Registered Financial Planner (RFP).

When selecting a financial planner also consider life experience. Using a 25-year-old to design a plan for a 60-year-old is probably a big mistake. A large age difference means differences in understanding financial priorities. A financial planner with similar life experience can pinpoint expenses and offset sources of income that a younger person may overlook. A financial plan prepared by someone who understands you will be more accurate and specific to your needs.

The next step

Update your financial plan every two to three years, to reflect changes in your life, and realities in the investment world. Fine tuning is necessary to keep it on track.

Financial planning starts the process. After that, you have to purchase the investments suggested in the plan.

Having a financial plan is like using a map to get to a destination. While it's no guarantee against losing your way, it helps get you back on course. With today's ocean of knowledge, a good financial plan is the best Rx (prescription) for information overload.

Classic investment advice from Fisher and Graham

The market is a voting machine, whereon countless individuals register choices which are the product partly of reason and partly of emotion.

Graham and Dodd

While many people consider Warren Buffet the greatest investor of our time, he freely credits his phenomenal investment success to the writings and tutelage of Philip Fisher and Ben Graham. Here is a review of Fisher's book *Common Stocks and Uncommon Profits*, and Graham's title *The Intelligent Investor*. Both of these books offer classic investment advice.

Common Stocks and Uncommon Profits, written by Philip Fisher in 1958, is considered an investment classic. Fisher survived and prospered after the great Depression. He also saw his investment strategies weather the second biggest financial storm of this century — the great bear market of 1974.

Since Fisher was a portfolio manager and not just a writer, his ideas faced the real world and were exposed to the worst of the market. Many of today's trendy investment books are written by people who don't have any practical experience managing money. Their pet theories haven't been tested by devastating market conditions.

In his book, Fisher highlighted 15 essential points that he believed a company must exhibit to be considered an outstanding investment opportunity. If the business missed many of these benchmarks, it was discarded for more favorable prospects.

Timeless advice is worth repeating, especially during periods when the markets are volatile and investors need to anchor themselves to strategies that work. Pick a stock that you are interested in or may already own and see how it stacks up against Fisher's selection criteria. Here are his 15 points:

1. Does the company have marketable products or services with sufficient market potential to make possible a sizeable increase in sales for at least several years?
2. Is management determined to developing products or processes that will increase total sales potentials when the growth potentials of current product lines have been exploited?
3. How effective are the company's research and development efforts in relation to its size?
4. Does the company have an above-average sales organization?
5. Does the company have a worthwhile profit margin?
6. What is the company doing to maintain or improve profit margins?
7. Does the company have outstanding labor and personnel relations?
8. Does the company have outstanding executive relations?
9. Does the company have depth to its management?
10. How good are the company's cost analysis and accounting controls?
11. Do peculiar aspects of the business make the company outstanding in relation to its competition?
12. Does the company have a short range or long range outlook to profits?
13. In the foreseeable future, will the company's growth require sufficient equity financing so that the larger number of outstanding shares will largely cancel the existing stockholders' benefit from the anticipated growth?

14. Does management talk freely to investors about its affairs when things are going well but "clam up" when troubles and disappointments occur?
15. Is the company's management of unquestionable integrity?

Fisher used this check list for over 50 years to determine the worthiness of potential investments. Spanning that period of time, his portfolio performance ranked far above that of his peers and over the market itself. Today, individuals can use this same format to screen the universe of common stocks for those that exhibit truly outstanding opportunity. If Warren Buffet can make $40 billion with this approach, it's worth a try.

Graham's seven criteria for selecting a portfolio of defensive common stocks

In his book *The Intelligent Investor*, Ben Graham describes a good investment as "one which upon thorough analysis promises safety of principal and an adequate rate of return. Operations not meeting these requirements are speculative." To avoid the catastrophic losses associated with undisciplined investing, Graham proposed a defensive investment strategy that focused exclusively on buying established companies with long records of profitable operations.

The specific criteria used by Graham to select a portfolio of defensive common stocks is worth repeating, especially in times of high volatility. In this market it's easy for even the most seasoned investor to lose his or her financial bearings.

Size

Bigger companies draw from greater financial resources. They can take advantage of business opportunities as they arise and weather economic storms that usually send many smaller companies to the grave. For industrial companies, Graham recommended that annual sales be at least $100 million. Utility stocks have sales of at least $50 million.

Finances

For industrial companies, current assets should be at least twice current liabilities. Long-term debt should not exceed the company's net current assets or working capital. For public utilities, debt should not exceed twice the company's stock equity. Debt-ridden companies are at a high risk should the economy falter or if interest rates rise dramatically.

Stability
The company should have been profitable for each of the past 10 years. A decade is enough to demonstrate whether a business can make money in good times and bad.

Dividends
A company's financial statements can easily be cooked. Dividends, however, don't lie. It's virtually impossible to pay out money to shareholders that you don't have. When a company consistently increases its dividend payouts, this is a quantifiable economic activity. Graham recommends a 20-year history of uninterrupted dividend payouts as a minimum criteria.

Earnings growth
At a minimum, a company should have increased its profits by 30 percent over the past decade. Since earnings are the ultimate driver of stock prices, the faster they grow, the higher the stocks price will tend to climb.

Price to earnings ratio (P.E.)
A stock's price to earnings ratio, or P.E., is the earnings per share that a company can generate, divided by its share price. It describes what price an investor has to pay for each dollar's worth of profits that a company generates. A share with a P.E. of 10 means that investors are willing to pay $10 for each dollar of profits. Graham recommended not paying more than 15 times a company's average earnings over the past three years.

Assets
In a world where the average North American stock is selling for five times the current value of its assets, Graham's seventh point stands out. He cautions that a company's current stock price should not be more than 1.5 times its last reported asset or book value.

Applying these seven criteria to the stock selection process will provide you with Ben Graham's "margin of safety." The more criteria the potential investment can satisfy, the less risky it becomes. While one can never eliminate all risk, following Graham's outline will certainly put the odds solidly in your favor.

Understanding bull and bear markets

Bear market — One that goes down.
Bull market — One that goes up.

In late 1996, Allan Greenspan, the influential head of the US Federal Reserve, called the speculative rush to purchase overpriced stocks "irrational exuberance." A prestigious Boston financial research firm in early 1998 soberly announced that at 29 times earnings, seven times asset value, and with a 1.5 percent dividend, stocks were at their highest valuation levels this century. Despite the warnings, investors provided the monetary fuel to keep share prices rocketing.

Suddenly in April 1998, the bull market that started back in 1991 derailed. The deepening economic crisis in Asia, Russia and Africa made people finally think about how they were investing their funds. Typical of the end of every economic boom, the psychological pendulum turned from unbridled greed to numbing fear.

The bear arrived and shredded stock prices with a vengeance. The third quarter of 1998 marked the worst performance the TSE 300 has seen since its statistical appearance in 1953. By August, the index had lost about 30 percent of its value.

Bear markets are essential to economic health

While a bear market mows a swath of financial and emotional duress, its periodic awakening is essential to both the long-term health of the economy and an investor's ability to build wealth through financial exposure to companies operating in that economy.

Bear markets are like the safety valve on a boiler. When excess pressure is at dangerous levels, the valve opens and provides an escape route. This prevents the system from exploding. Bear markets take the speculative excesses out of financial assets by returning them to price levels that more accurately reflect their true value.

The expression "the higher they go, the harder they fall" describes an unchecked economy. It will rise to heights from which a fall will be permanently devastating unless restrained. Periodic bear markets keep speculative bubbles from reaching the critical mass necessary to trigger financial cataclysm. They are a vital sign that shows that an economy is healthy enough to resist the occasional bout of financial flu.

Bear markets put stocks back into the hands of their rightful owners

Rapidly rising share prices bring hoards of unsophisticated investors into the market. This puts business ownership into the hands of people who are looking for quick speculative gains instead of those seeking to build long-term positions in profitable companies. A healthy business can't be built on the premise of hot money that is here today and gone tomorrow. Corporations require extended time to turn investment capital into profits. This can only be done when the majority of investors give a company use of their capital for a long time. With scared speculators heading for the hills, stock ownership is once again being transferred back into the hands of its rightful owners.

Bear markets are a reality check

It is believed that bull markets will continue forever and provide endless profits. Surveys show that 90 percent of those in the market today, including fund managers, have never seen a bear market prior to 1998. With such inexperience, these babes have no concept of risk and even less knowledge of good, long-term investment performance. People are shocked when they hear that over the last two centuries, the stock market has provided a real or after inflation return of 6.9 percent per year. Recent polling shows that investors expect real returns of more than 25 percent per annum.

There is no free lunch

Anyone who is a seasoned investor has been humbled repeatedly by strategies that don't pan out, even though they were exhaustively and thoroughly researched. Most novice equity players today have no feel for the hard work and discipline that is required or the investment selection process. Since virtually everything has been rising in price over the last few years, it's been a snap to make money without having to pay attention to basic company fundamentals like asset quality, management expertise, profitability, growth prospects and relative value. The days of making easy money are definitely over. Most casual investors will shift their money back into GICs, leaving a much less crowded field for the disciplined long-term players who know that the task of wealth building brings no free lunch.

A bear market has a silver lining
Bear markets don't continue forever. In fact, their average duration since the beginning of the century has been less than 18 months. In the year following the market bottom of every bad market since 1950, the average rise in stock prices has been an amazing 30 percent. Unless you believe we are headed for an unrecoverable crash, use a bear market's weakness to purchase cheap assets before the crowds figure it out and rush back in to buy the same things at higher prices. Think of a bear market as a large department store with merchandise available at a 30 percent discount.

CHAPTER 7

BUILDING AN INCOME PRODUCING PORTFOLIO

- A buyer's guide to income trusts
- On bonds, budgets and free lunches
- Investing for US income
- Laddering your way to financial success
- Convertible securities offer low risk and high returns
- Fixed income strategies for RRSP investments

People should be more concerned with the return of their principal than the return on their principal.
Will Rogers

The safest way to double your money is to fold it over once and put it in your pocket.
Kim Hibbard

If you don't know who you are, the stock market is an expensive place to find out.
George Goodman

Wall Street's graveyards are filled with men who were right too soon.
William Hamilton

A buyer's guide to income trusts

Gone are the days when an investor could walk into any financial institution and buy a guaranteed investment certificate with a rate of interest of 10 percent plus. Today, returns are so low that even 30-year Government of Canada bonds yield six percent. Anyone creating a portfolio of higher income paying investments in today's environment must look beyond risk free securities to achieve a reasonable return.

ITU (income trust units) offer a higher rate of return. An ITU is a business that's structured to pay out profits to shareholders on a monthly or quarterly basis. Recent initial public offerings of income trust units have offered projected yields ranging from eight percent to 10 percent or higher.

Are ITUs safe?

Like any investment, ITUs are available in a variety of industries that cover the spectrum of investment quality and risk. Most of the income trust units currently offered fall into the following categories:

Utilities. Income trusts in this category either generate electricity or are pipelines that transport oil and gas. Their predictable nature generally makes them quite conservative.

Real estate. Real estate investment trusts (REIT) hold portfolios of income producing properties including strip malls, office towers, residential apartments, hotels and motels, retirement and nursing homes and even storage facilities. Most REITs fall in the low to medium risk category.

Manufacturing and distribution. This type of trust unit includes businesses like port facilities, fuel processing plants, fuel distribution centers, and various other manufacturing enterprises. Sensitive to the economic cycle, these ITUs are in the medium risk category.

Mining and energy. ITUs in this category produce oil and gas or minerals like coal or iron ore. The volatile nature of commodity prices and depleting resources make these securities a high risk investment.

What are the risks of ITUs?

ITUs are not in the same category as guaranteed investment certificates. Unlike fixed income securities, income trust units have no fixed rate of return, maturity date, or known terminal value. As operating companies that suffer from rising and falling profits, this can lead to fluctuating levels of income. As income driven instruments, their market prices will naturally be sensitive to the rise and fall of interest rates. As a result, they will move in price much like bonds. If interest rates start to climb, the market value of most ITUs will probably start to drop. Investors unable to tolerate price volatility shouldn't purchase income trust units. The recent market gyration in trust unit prices should be enough to give any GIC refugee pause for thought.

The features and benefits of ITUs

High cash flow. As non-taxable entities, ITUs are required to pay out all income to unit holders that's not needed by the business to meet normal operating expenses. Most companies that are transformed into income trusts don't have a high need for capital to expand and grow. As a result, they can direct the majority of their profits towards shareholder's wallets.

Tax deferral or tax reduction. Some ITUs pay out income in the form of dividends which are eligible for favorable tax treatment. Many ITUs also pay out a large portion of their cash flow which Revenue Canada considers a return of capital. This type of income isn't taxable upon receipt, but is added on the unit's price at the point of sale and is taxed as a capital gain at that time. Income that's treated as a return of capital will be taxed when the investment is sold. In many cases, this means an investor can defer paying tax on a large amount of income for many years. Since this income is treated as a capital gain, it also qualifies for a much lower tax rate.

Income trust units can be ideal for cash-strapped investors looking for high income and significant tax advantages. They are however, not intended as a substitute for guaranteed, fixed-term investments.

On budgets, bonds and free lunches

1995 will go down in history as the year Canadians finally came to grips with government debt. By the end of the 1999 all the provinces except Quebec and B.C. will be showing balanced budgets. More amazing still, the Federal government, for the first time in three decades, actually CUT spending. They did it without reverting to their old tax-the-middle-class strategy.

Now the bad news! At the Federal government's rate, it will take 10 years to balance the budget and another 20 years to pay off the debt. Even so, if the government has the political courage to stay with its deficit reduction program, the long-term direction of interest rates is DOWN. However, over the next few years, there will be volatility in rates as the government grapples to get spending under control. This will be heaven for those people who have both the financial tools and strategies to understand the impact.

The attraction of bonds

Many financial instruments can be used to profit from interest rate swings. Two of the most popular, for the average investor, are bonds and strip coupons. Both are defined as a debt obligation between two parties where one party lends the other money in return for a negotiated rate of return and a guarantee that the original investment will be paid back at a specific date in the future. They can be issued by both governments and corporations and come in a variety of maturity dates. The main difference between the two is that bonds usually pay out interest twice a year, whereas strip coupons let the interest compound and only pay it back along with the principal on the maturity date. Both of these investments, ideal for the strategy outlined below, are easily traded through a brokerage firm. Few people realize that the bond market in Canada is 39 times larger than the stock market.

A strategy that works

To make money trading bonds and strip coupons, purchase them when interest rates are high and sell them when interest rates are low. The logic: bond and strip coupon prices fall when interest rates rise and go up as interest rates descend. There is a simple reason for this formula. Imagine that you bought a bond that came due in 10 years and had an interest rate of 10 percent per year. Now let's assume that the interest rate rose to 15 percent. In this higher interest rate environment, you would have a difficult time trying to sell your bond. After all, why would anyone want to buy a bond paying 10 percent when the current rate was five percent higher. The only way to liquidate your bond position would be to keep lowering the price until it became cheap enough to makeup for the five percent difference in interest rates. In real life, this would mean dropping your $1,000 priced bond down to $745.13.

Now let's reverse the example and assume that after you bought the 10-year bond paying 10 percent, interest rates fell to five percent. If you tried to sell your bond in this environment, you'd be treated like a hero instead of a leper. In this case, everyone would want a bond guaranteeing a high rate of 10 percent, especially for a 10-year term. In fact, because your bond was paying five percent more than the going rate, you could command a premium. Once again, in real life, you'd be able to sell your bond for $1,389.73 or about 39 percent more than the purchase price.

The reward is a free lunch

Investing in bonds and coupons is a win-win situation. If rates drop, trade your bonds for a profit. If interest rates stay the same or go up, don't trade them. Keep them until maturity and collect your annual interest. In the investment world, this is the closest thing you'll ever find to a free lunch.

Investing for US income

Since Canada's stock and bond markets account for about three percent of the world's total, limiting yourself exclusively to the Great White North eliminates 97 percent of other investments. To increase your global exposure why not consider investing in our giant neighbor south of the 49th parallel?

The United States accounts for 38 percent of global investment opportunities. Although this nation has domestic problems, it represents a rich and economically diverse country. Here is a review of the many options available to the investor looking for securities producing income in US dollars.

Seek US income for tax savings

Many Canadian companies issue preferred shares which pay dividends in US dollars. These shares are purchased with American money. The quarterly income payments qualify for the dividend tax credit. Dividends receive preferential tax treatment.

To compare dividend yields to interest yields, multiply the dividend yield by 1.272. Using an example of the Canadian Imperial Bank of Commerce preferred, multiply its dividend yield of 5.5 percent by 1.27 to calculate an interest equivalent of seven percent. It takes seven percent in interest income to derive the same after tax return in Alberta as a 5.5 percent dividend.

How to choose US income with RRSP eligibility

Over the last few years considerable domestic financing has been done in the form of bonds issued in foreign currency. These securities pay interest and also give repayment of principal upon maturity in that foreign currency. Since these bonds are 100 percent RRSP eligible, they are especially attractive.

Also, as they are guaranteed by a Canadian institution, Revenue Canada does not consider them as foreign content, although they are denominated in foreign currency and pay interest in foreign currency. This means that 100 percent of the value of an RRSP can be put in foreign denominated bonds of a Canadian issuer without triggering the 20 percent foreign content limit. Canadian bonds denominated in US dollars can currently be purchased with yields exceeding six percent.

Choose income that is guaranteed by the US government

Because of our government's financial incompetence, many individuals want their money guaranteed by a government or corporation that is non-Canadian. Any brokerage firm with a good foreign bond desk can accommodate you. As the world's largest borrower, numerous US government, guaranteed bonds are available.

How to get income plus growth

The US market contains many profitable companies which regularly pay out a large portion of profits in dividends. These stocks provide cash flow which can be used to finance your stay at that ocean side condominium in Florida. Over time, they will generally increase in value.

Consider American utility stocks. Many pay dividends of over five percent. Utility companies are partially government regulated and provide an essential service. Therefore, they are a safer way to participate in the US stock market. Since their profits are predictable, they represent an excellent venue for the investor wanting a conservative income producing stock with some growth potential. Over the long-term, US utility stocks have produced a total return exceeding 12 percent per year.

Whether you're concerned about our current economic and political situation or looking for a way to finance your winter vacation, Uncle Sam has many investments to meet your needs.

Laddering your way to financial success

After accumulating enough money to make an RRSP contribution, the next step is deciding how to invest the cash. Revenue Canada says that all investment gain within an RRSP grows tax free until withdrawal from the plan. At that time, any withdrawals are added to income and taxed accordingly. Considering taxation, here are some suggestions on buying investments for your RRSP.

Buy stocks outside RRSPs

Over the last 30 years, the long-term rates of return on stocks in Canada and bonds have been virtually the same. The gains from both asset classes are taxed identically when withdrawn from the RRSP. Therefore, the marginally higher returns that stock ownership offers inside an RRSP don't justify the extra risk.

Carefully consider where you own your stocks. They make the most tax sense being held outside the RRSP. Stocks can increase in value (capital gains) and may pay out cash to the stockholder (dividends). Both capital gains and dividends are eligible for considerable tax savings over a comparable amount of interest income. Outside an RRSP, the 10 percent extra return that stocks have over bonds grows to about a 40 percent advantage when tax is considered. Thus, a general rule of thumb, buy stocks outside the RRSP and fixed income investments inside the RRSP.

How to achieve good cash flow

If you agree with this logic so far, then you should consider a strategy for fixed income investment inside an RRSP called laddering. Laddering is simply staggering the maturity dates on interest bearing investments so they all don't come due at the same time. This technique overcomes two problems. Firstly, it eliminates the hit and miss process of trying to pick the top of the interest rate cycle. Secondly, it removes the guesswork of calculating annual cash flows after retirement.

A recent study by Legg and Mason showed that economists were only right about 30 percent of the time when asked to predict the direction and movement of interest rates over the upcoming six months. This statistic isn't given to knock economists, but rather to show the futility of trying to crystal ball interest rates. If these people, with their computer models and staffs of Ph.D.s can't do it, there isn't much hope for mere mortals like you and I.

Laddering allows you to get around the thorny problem of interest rate guesstimation as the strategy is built around the concept of averaging. Because you are staggering the maturity dates of your investments, you are never totally exposing yourself to abnormally high or low rates.

Secondly, laddering allows the retiring person to know exactly what annual cash flow they will have in the future. Let's assume that you and your spouse are 60 years old and have a total of $250,000 in your combined RRSPs. In this case, you're looking for an annual income until the age of 80 since you're not leaving an estate, and you want to exhaust the accumulated principal along with the interest over the next 20 years. A solution: divide the money and ladder it into strip coupons with one maturing every year for the next 20 years. By investing this way, you'll know your annual retirement income, to the last penny.

If you have fixed income investments in your RRSP, consider laddering as an essential tool in your climb towards financial success.

Convertible securities offer low risk and high return

When most people think about convertibles they envision middle-aged men reliving their youth, warm summer days and long blonde hair blowing in the breeze. In the financial world, we're talking about investments rather than ragtops.

Convertible bonds or debentures, as they're known in the financial world, are an investment hybrid. These investments combine the income of a bond with a stock's growth potential.

Convertible bonds are issued in multiples of $1,000, usually with a fixed rate of interest paid twice a year. Their biggest safety feature is a maturity date when the issuer promises to pay back the convertible bond holder's original investment amount in cash or with the equivalent amount of common shares.

Convertible bonds are exchangeable into a specific number of an issuing company's common shares — hence, the name convertible. If the common share's value rises, so does the convertible.

The return is usually better than a common share

Convertible bonds are especially attractive for the conservative investor. The income they pay is usually superior to that of a common share, yet they have the growth potential that a straight bond can't deliver.

Statistical research shows that convertibles do better in lousy markets than do the underlying common shares they represent and almost as well as in good markets.

Should the issuing company have financial troubles which lead to bankruptcy or insolvency, convertible bonds offer a degree of safety. Convertibles are usually issued so the holder has a claim on the general credit worthiness of the company. If the worst happens, then convertible holders stand in line after Revenue Canada, employees and creditors who have claims on specific assets. However, they come before preferred and common shareholders. If a company is forced to liquidate its assets, convertible holders have a better chance of getting all or part of their money back than do holders of stock.

Convertibles are also a good choice for individuals wanting a low risk way to participate in the stock market. An investor can collect a nice rate of return while waiting for the underlying stock's value to climb. If the shares do well, the investor can convert the bonds into a specific number of common shares or sell the convertible for a profit. Should the stock do nothing, or drop in value, the investor could keep the bond until maturity and collect its stated rate of return. These options make convertibles about the closest thing ever devised to fulfilling the Holy Grail of the investment world — higher returns without higher risks.

The new kid on the block

Since convertibles represented a very small market in Canada, most people are unfamiliar with them. In recent years, convertibles have become popular as an alternate way for corporations to raise money. The public has demanded the product. Today, there are over 60 issues trading in Canada with a market value of over $7 billion. In 1994, there were over 10 major issues brought to market with a value of $1.7 billion.

The convertible market is no longer obscure. Household names including Roger's Communications, Inco, MacMillan Bloedel, Air Canada and Luscar all issue convertibles.

Since convertible securities are considerably more complex than either stocks or bonds, they demand a much higher level of expertise from the investor. They offer a profitable return and a low risk way to participate in today's volatile capital markets.

Convertibles are about as close as it gets to being the perfect investment.

Fixed income strategies for RRSP investments

Interest rates haven't been this low since the early '60s. This is great if you have to borrow money, but tragic if you're trying to find a conservative investment for your RRSP. Since most RRSP contributions find a home in interest bearing investments, here are some fixed income strategies that address the current low rate environment.

Strategy 1 — Keep your money short-term and wait for opportunity

Interest rates in Canada are volatile. In 1992, for example, short-term interest rates bottomed out at about five percent. Three months later, the same rates were over nine percent. In 1994, rates dropped below five percent. Within months, they doubled. In both cases, the experts said interest rates would probably stay at those depressed levels for years.

Rates are now below five percent. Will they defy recent history and stay low for an extended period? Will they follow the previous trends? Will an unstable currency and a heated political climate push rates even higher later this year?

If you subscribe to theory B, the preferred strategy would be to purchase liquid short-term investments like money market funds, treasury bills or 30 to 90-day investment certificates. Then wait for the next interest rate explosion and lock in for the longer term.

Strategy 2 — Invest long-term

Usually, the longer the term, the higher the rate. Investors have to be adequately compensated with a better return for investing money for longer periods. Currently 15-year provincial bonds pay about one percent more than their one-year counterparts. For those needing a higher rate of return now, buying longer term is an obvious solution. However, if rates should rise, you can only capture the higher rates by selling the previously purchased investments at a loss.

Strategy 3 — Find investments with lower credit ratings
Before a corporation or government borrows money, credit agencies exhaustively evaluate their credit worthiness. This credit rating determines the interest rate at which they can borrow money on the bond market.

With a low credit rating, lenders demand a higher interest rate. For example, interest rates on Swiss debt or bonds is one percentage point lower than similar Canadian debt. This in turn, is half a percent lower than Quebec debt, which is two percentage points lower than Cambridge Shopping Centres (a real estate company) debt, which is one percent lower than Luscar debt which currently yields around nine percent. In each case, as the credit quality drops, the yield or interest rates rise. Investment dealers specializing in bond trading sell high yielding bonds.

Strategy 4 — Grit your teeth and jump in
If you're not concerned about today's interest rates, invest for three to five years. Currently, investments with these maturities are offering yields of about six percent. At this rate, money doubles in 12 years. While this doesn't equate to knock-your-socks-off-performance, with inflation at only 1.5 percent, it provides a real (after inflation) return of four percent. Historically, over the last 70 years, the real return on fixed income investments was only two percent, so it makes a four percent return look turbo charged.

Strategy 5 — Look at other types of investments
For those willing to venture beyond the safe haven of interest bearing investments, an entire galaxy of stocks and mutual funds promise higher returns. Since 1970, the Canadian stock market has plodded along at a respectable 10 percent per year. International stock markets have done better, averaging between 12 percent and 14 percent per annum. Just remember, with increased reward comes increased risk. Translation: unless you are willing to sit through times when your investment drops in value by 25 to 30 percent, don't get involved.

You can wait, take higher risks, increase the term, find fixed income alternatives or ignore the low rates and invest anyway. Your strategy is determined by your patience and your risk tolerance.

CHAPTER 8

WINNING MUTUAL FUND STRATEGIES

- Buying the unloved can be profitable
- If mutual funds are the answer, here are the questions
- Seven steps to picking mutual funds with killer performance and low risk
- Closed-end funds are your opportunity to buy stocks for 75 cents on the dollar

If you don't profit from your investment mistakes, someone else will.

Yale Hirsch

The stock market is that creation of man which humbles him the most.

Anonymous

Lack of money is the root of all evil.

George Bernard Shaw

The price of a stock varies inversely with the thickness of its research file.

Martin T. Sosnoff

Buying the unloved can be profitable

Mutual fund investors seem to regularly make the tragic mistake of pouring money into the biggest winner of the previous 12 months. History has repeatedly shown that purchasing last year's Dr. Jekyll often reveals this year's Mr. Hyde.

Morningstar, a respected US mutual fund rating agency, has done extensive research on the dynamics of mutual fund performance. Their statistical work on the "hot" fund phenomenon is especially enlightening. The results suggest that an investor may want to rethink the selection criteria for mutual funds.

Every year, *Morningstar Fund Investor* picks the three most "unpopular" fund categories of the previous 12 months. Their definition of unloved is based on the percentage change of cash going into or out of funds in each category or sector. After the overall categories are chosen, Morningstar then recommends investing in one specific fund from each of the three broad categories for a period of three years. The results of this investment strategy, which have been back tested to 1987, illustrate that the industry's ugly ducklings have a 78 percent chance of beating the average equity fund over a three-year period and a 89 percent chance of outperforming the most popular funds. Over the decade long span of the study, the previous year's most popular funds showed an average return of 9.4 percent, while the supposed 97-pound weaklings generated a return that averaged 15.5 percent per year. The unwanted and unloved group of funds outperformed the glamour boys by an amazing six percent per year.

While the results seem puzzling, the logic of this successful process isn't a mystery. Like any investment strategy, the premise of profit is "buy low and sell high." Buy assets when they're out of favor and cheap. Then sell those same assets when they're overly loved and overly priced. The same principles apply to mutual funds. Individual funds with sizzling performance numbers usually have a portfolio of assets that have appreciated substantially and are likely overpriced. As a rule, funds with rates of return that are under water have unwanted and unloved securities that are trading at depressingly low prices. As with stocks, the only way to make money is to adhere to the obvious — buy low and sell high.

While this is a US study based on American mutual funds, the results challenge conventional wisdom, especially the notion that chasing a small group of funds with hot performance numbers is a winning strategy.

Based on the previous study, what should an investor buy if he or she is looking for funds that would be winners over three years? According to *Morningstar Fund Investor's* year end numbers, sectors in Latin America and Asia/Pacific markets experienced the highest outflow of capital. Right now, these markets look inviting.

A word of caution before implementing the above strategy. To make it work, you must be willing to buy when others are selling. Conversely, you must sell when everyone is buying. This takes an unwavering conviction to stay the course. This is why so few people are wealthy.

If mutual funds are the answer, here are the questions

Mutual funds are sold on the basis of performance numbers that are often more hype than fact. Before making your next fund purchase, take this test. You'll find the results enlightening.

1. How many mutual funds have averaged a 20 percent or better annual compound return over the last 10 years? (Hint: only 500 funds have been around for 10 years.)
   a. 10 b. 30 c. 0 d. 60

2. How many mutual funds have averaged a 15 percent or better annual compound return over the last 10 years?
   a. 90 b. 110 c. 4 d. 21

3. How many mutual funds have averaged a 12 percent or better annual compound return over the last 10 years?
   a. 204 b. 69 c. 67 d. 39

4. How well has the average mutual fund done over the last 10 years in terms of annual compound return?
   a. 11% b. 10% c. 8.1% d. 7%

5. What kind of annual return have the worst 10 performing funds achieved over 10 years?
a. 9% b. -1% c. 3% d. -4%

6. Over the last 10 years, mutual funds that bought Canadian stocks averaged three percent better performance per year than the money market funds?
a. true b. false

7. Over the past 10 years, domestic bond funds performed about the same as mutuals investing in the Canadian stock market?
a. true b. false

8. Over the last 10 years, the average Asian equity fund has outperformed the average US equity (stock) fund?
a. true b. false

9. The average Asian equity fund over 10 years has achieved what kind of annual return?
a. 3% b. 16% c. 7% d. 12%

10. Over the last 10 years, the average US equity mutual fund has produced what kind of annual return?
a. 7.6% b. 9.4% c. 13.8% d. 18.5%

11. What percentage of funds that invest in the Canadian stock market could outperform the TSE 35 Index over the last one year?
a. 46% b. 13% c. 66% d. 30%

12. What percentage of funds that invest in the Canadian stock market could outperform the TSE 35 Index over the last three years?
a. 28% b. 12% c. 73% d. 49%

13. What percentage of funds that invest in the Canadian stock market outperformed the TSE 35 Index over the last five years?
a. 10% b. 29% c. 41% d. 17%

14. Which strategy gives you the best return over a five-year period?
a. buying the five worst performing funds each year
b. buying the five best performing funds each year

Answers

1. c
2. d
3. b
4. c
5. d
6. b
7. a
8. b
9. a
10. c
11. a
12. a
13. d
14. a

Total your score. Several conclusions can be drawn from these results:

1. The majority of mutual funds cannot outperform the overall market;
2. Over the last decade, most Canadian stock funds barely beat the performance of bond funds;
3. Although the average stock fund barely outperformed bond funds over a 10-year period, they also took on much more risk.

Considering these facts, many people might be discouraged from buying mutual funds. Long-term performance stats show that they aren't the magical road to riches.

However, top performing funds are the exception. Search through the marketing rubble and you can find them. By doing your homework you'll avoid the marketing hype and be rewarded with true performance.

Seven steps to picking mutual funds with killer performance and low risk

The ultimate goal of every investor should be to achieve a high a rate of return while taking low risk. This seven-step guide shows you how to select equity mutual funds (the ones that buy stocks) that are long on performance and short on risk.

Step 1 — Beware the smell of diapers

The average mutual fund manager has been at his or her trade for a meager three and one-half years. This could have negative implications for mutual investors who trust babes to manage their money.

Any seasoned manager has a profound respect for stock market risks, as he or she has watched 25 percent to 35 percent of a large mutual fund's value disappear into the black hole of a bear market. These rollercoaster riders know the importance of avoiding the panicky, knee-jerk reactions which follow in the aftermath.

Unfortunately, most of the managers in diapers have never experienced or learned the lessons from the financial and emotional bludgeoning of a bear market. Prior to 1998, the last major market massacre was in 1987, a year when many of these investment managers were finishing high school. You don't want a novice fund manager learning the business at your expense.

Always remember! When it comes to managing other people's money, there can never be too much experience. When markets are hot, even a monkey throwing darts at a newspaper listing of stocks will likely pick several winners. However, amidst fear and panic, a manager with 20 years experience can ride the storm.

Step 2 — Avoid Revenue Canada's favorite funds

Performance doesn't equate to what you make, but rather, what you keep after expenses and taxes. Unfortunately, every time a mutual fund manager sells a position in his or her portfolio, it triggers a buy or a sell fee from the broker that completed the transaction. These fees add to the cost of managing your money which directly affects your performance. The higher the costs, the lower the returns.

In addition, whenever a stock is sold for a profit, Revenue Canada says tax must be paid on the gains. Higher trading leads to higher taxes. If more money goes into Revenue Canada's coffers, less will be compounding in yours. Funds with little trading have a low turnover ratio. All things being equal, a fund with a low turnover ratio usually gives an investor a superior rate of after tax return than a fund with the same performance, but a high turnover ratio. The ultimate selection criteria for picking a fund is what's left in your pocket (net after tax returns). Low turnover funds are the smart investor's choice in taxable accounts.

Step 3 — Put the money where the mouth is

An individual invests differently when his or her personal money is risked alongside yours. A fund manager with a large portion of his or her personal net worth invested in the assets they manage, shows a healthy self interest in good performance and risk avoidance. Warren Buffet, Martin Zweig, Peter Cundill, John Templeton and Charles Brandes are all renowned for managing funds that continually produce high returns with low volatility. Not surprisingly, these individuals all have considerable personal wealth invested in the same investments as their clients. If a fund manager isn't willing to put his money where his mouth is, why should you?

Step 4 — Don't buy yesterday's news

The results of a recent Towers Perrin study tracking the returns of the 80 biggest Canadian money managers, showed that after a four-year period of generating top quartile results, a manager had just over 40 percent probability of generating above average performance. Conversely, the likelihood of above average performance after four years of poor results was 60 percent.

Other research suggests that as a fund's one-year rate of return rises, so does the likelihood of it being in the bottom quartile in performance the following year.

Clearly a strategy of picking last year's winners usually means you're buying this year's losers.

Step 5 — Look for the Steady Eddies

The *Globe and Mail* publishes a monthly total return spread sheet on most of the major mutual funds in Canada. Fund performance is broken down into one-month, three-month, six-month, one-year, five-year and 10-year periods. This table gives a realistic snapshot on the consistency of differing fund's returns over varying periods of time. Using this tool, an investor can look for funds that show steady returns, from the short to the longer term.

Most people should invest the bulk of their portfolio in Steady Eddies because 90 percent of mutual fund investors aren't aggressive risk takers. If they buy a volatile fund, that subsequently goes down in price, they will automatically sell it. This knee jerk reaction is why the typical mutual fund investor has so little to show in the way of returns for the risks they take. Jumping in and out of funds, while trying to be a market timer doesn't work. Since most people find it virtually impossible to resist switching out of a volatile fund once it's gone down, the best strategy is not to buy it in the first place. Steady Eddies, because of their consistency, give the average investor enough comfort to resist lemming-like urges to buy high and sell low. As a result, the fund has time to generate consistent long-term returns.

Step 6 — Avoid one day wonders

Money management is big business. Top portfolio managers make millions of dollars a year in salary and are actively courted by the competition like a top athlete. Stealing from the competition's nest makes for a transitory place to work. Investment professionals are akin to gunslingers in the old west who lent their services to the highest taker.

Unfortunately, funds with a high management turnover cost you money. A new manager will buy and sell securities to match his or her investment views. These trades create transaction costs which directly come out of your pocket.

Secondly, the portfolio is static during the transition period between an old manager's departure and a new one's arrival. Time may be required to fine tune the portfolio. There may be extended intervals with little or no performance.

Step 7 — Return is only half of the equation

The Holy Grail of investing is to achieve a high level of return, while taking a low level of risk. Your job as an investor is to find fund managers who can achieve this goal. To do this, obtain an issue of the *Globe and Mail* containing the monthly mutual fund performance statistics.

The first column uses a series of stars to rank funds according to their rate of return. One star represents the lowest ranking and five stars the highest. The second column rates funds according to their volatility or risk, either low, average or highly volatile.

To create a list of "low risk/high return" funds, work your way down the volatility column and highlight funds with a low volatility rating. Further screen these remaining funds and pick only those with a four-star performance rating.

Systematically apply these criteria

Further screen the short list. Apply criteria one through six. You should find four or five finalists that'll both delight you with their performance and pacify you with their stability.

Closed-end funds are your opportunity to buy stocks for 75 cents on the dollar

If you're looking for bargains in the stock market, then you need to take a close look at a little known type of security called a closed-end mutual fund.

A mutual fund is a pool of investor money. This cash is invested by professional managers. Mutuals are either open or closed-end. The buy and sell price of an open ended fund is directly determined by the value of the fund's underlying investments. Purchases and sales are made directly with the fund based on that day's asset value.

A closed-end fund differs from its cousin in the way that its units are bought and sold. The closed-end fund has shares that are listed on a stock exchange. Investors trade these shares in the market instead of buying and selling them directly with the mutual fund company. The price of a closed-end fund is determined by what people are willing to pay for the shares and not what the asset value is on any given day.

Depending on market conditions, a closed-end fund's price may be below its portfolio's net asset value per share (a discount) or above it (a premium). Because a closed-end fund's shares can trade above or below their current asset value, there is'a fertile field of opportunity awaiting any investor. Investors buying closed-end funds can profit in two ways. Firstly, if the fund's portfolio increases in value, the share price will rise. Secondly, if the fund's investment success is received enthusiastically by optimistic investors, the demand for the fund can lessen the discount that the share price is trading in relation to its asset value per share or can even push the share price to a premium.

Consider, for example, a fund with a $10 per share asset value currently trading at $8 per share. If a good market boosts the net asset value of the fund by 20 percent to $12 per share and at the same time enthusiastic investors bid up the fund's shares enough to eliminate the discount, the market price of the shares would also rise to $12. The $4 increase would represent a 50 percent gain from the $8 initial market price. In arithmetic terms, the share price of the closed-end fund would have risen two times as much as the fund's net asset value.

Seth Copeland Anderson, a finance professor at the University of Alabama, published an amazing study done in 1985 in the *Journal of Portfolio Management* on such a strategy. In his study

Dr. Anderson bought 17 closed-end mutual funds at a 25 percent discount to net asset value per share and sold them when the discount shrank to 10 percent. This strategy had returns 6.8 times better than the US stock market, as a whole, between 1965-1969, 1.25 times better returns between 1969 and 1976 and 3.2 times better returns between 1977 and 1984.

To effectively invest in closed-end funds a person needs to have quality information on discounts and premiums to asset value. Two good places to look for this information are *Barron's* and the *National Post*. Next, make a list of eligible candidates currently exceeding the 25 percent discount threshold.

Once the strategy feels comfortable, then purchase five to eight funds with a 25 percent or more discount. Hold them until the discount shrinks to under 10 percent, then sell. A consistent application of this strategy over the long-term should provide very pleasing results.

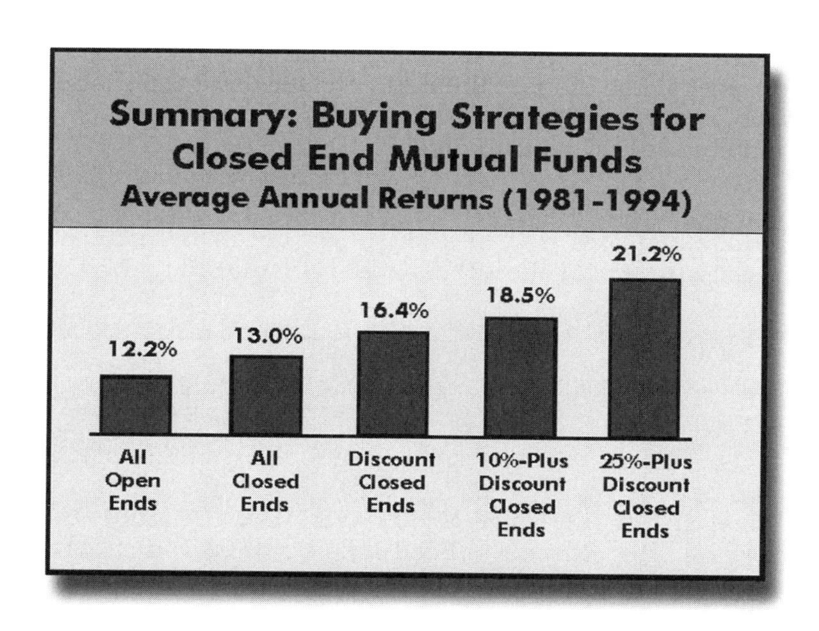

CHAPTER 9

WISE WAYS TO INVEST IN THE STOCK MARKET

- Value investing — the key to high reward with low risk
- The other half — selling
- A junior stock shopping guide
- How good are your trading skills?
- Widow and orphan stocks can help you make your $1 million
- A stock buyer's check list

Buy on rumor, sell on the news.

Anonymous

Always sell what shows you a loss and keep what shows you a gain.

Jesse Livermore

Every crowd has a silver lining.

P.T. Barnum

Value investing — the key to high reward with low risk

Spend at least as much time researching a stock as you would to choose a refrigerator.
Peter Lynch

For many people, value investing is a mystery. However, if you can find bargains at the grocery store, then you have the necessary skills to find value stocks. A bargain at the supermarket is a high quality item at the cheapest price. This is also the value investing strategy. Value stocks have the following characteristics:

- low stock price to book value;
- low stock price to earnings (P.E.);
- higher than average dividend payout.

Find stocks that fit as many of these criteria as possible. You'll have a higher margin of safety owning a stock when it meets most of these guidelines. You'll also prosper financially. Here is an explanation of the criteria.

Low stock price to book value

To obtain the price to book value, divide the total value of a company's assets (as shown on its books) by the number of outstanding shares. To derive the book value per share, divide this number by the market price of one share of the company's stock.

You are trying to determine the dollar amount of assets represented by each share of the company. The higher the dollar value of the assets backing each share, the cheaper the stock. While it's advantageous to buy a dollar's worth of assets for 50 cents, in today's market, a good bargain can be any stock trading at or below 1.5 times book value per share.

Low stock price to earnings (P.E.)

Divide a company's earnings by the total number of outstanding shares to derive its earnings per share. Divide this number into the current price of the stock to calculate the P.E., or price earnings multiple. This ratio gives you an idea of how expensive a stock is in comparison to its current earnings. For example, if a stock was priced at $100 and had a dollar's worth of earnings per share, then the stock would be trading at 100 times this year's earnings.

Companies trading at less than 10 times earnings are bargains. In this hot market, companies at less than 15 times earnings can present some intriguing opportunities.

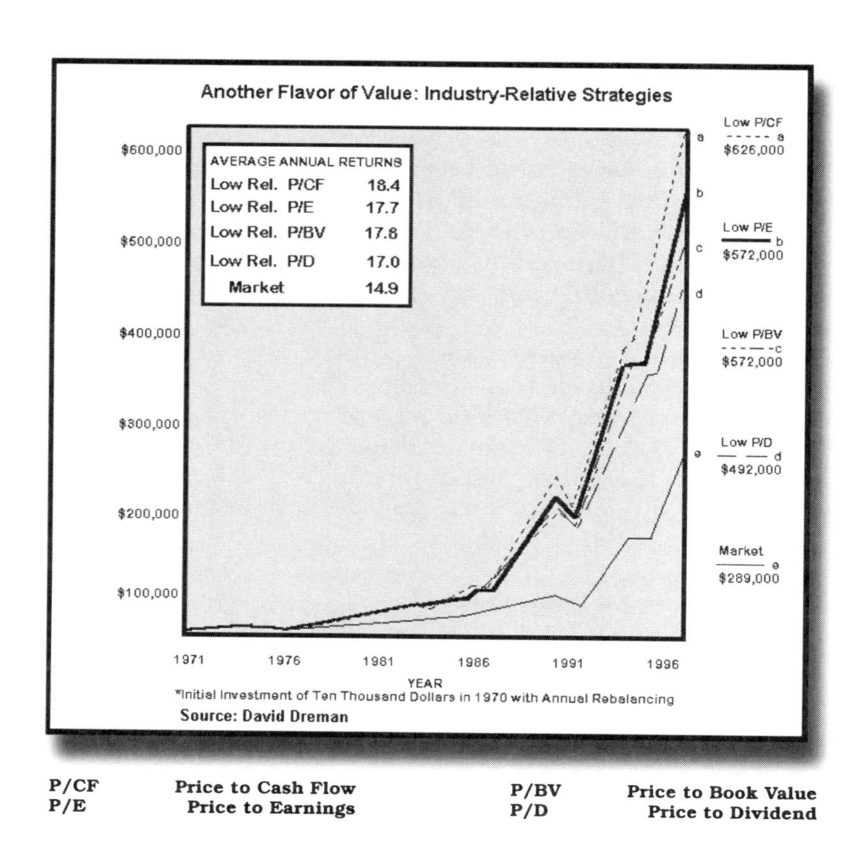

P/CF **Price to Cash Flow** **P/BV** **Price to Book Value**
P/E **Price to Earnings** **P/D** **Price to Dividend**

Higher than average dividend payout

A dividend is any cash a company takes out of its earnings to pay to shareholders. This is usually paid quarterly in the form of a cheque.

Today, the average Toronto or New York listed stock is paying a dividend of about two percent. Considering current market conditions, any stock paying a 3.5 percent dividend or better (without abnormally high levels of debt) is a value candidate. When looking for dividend paying stocks, finding companies that pay high relative dividends is an advantage. However, finding businesses with higher than normal dividends and a long track record of yearly increases in those dividends is an investor's version of having died and gone to heaven.

Putting it all together

A recent study by Frank Russell conducted between 1979 and 1995, shows that for smaller companies a value approach to investing outperformed buying high priced growth stocks. The returns of 17.2 percent versus 12.6 percent per year is even more remarkable considering that the value approach involved 30 percent less risk or volatility than the growth approach to investing.

The next time someone tells you that you have to take higher risks to get higher returns, show them the stats. Low risk value stocks historically have generated better returns than their high risk high growth counterparts. Who says life is fair?

The other half — selling

Few "how to pick stock" articles talk about selling them. Few give the other half of the equation. Making money requires both buying and selling. Profits are only paper until a security is sold. Unless an investor wants to enter into a "death-do-us-part" relationship, selling is an important, albeit neglected, investment skill. Here are some reasons why you may want to consider selling your investments.

Rebalancing your portfolio reduces risk

To reduce exposure to any one security, a single investment shouldn't represent more than 10 percent of the portfolio's total value. However, because of the recent seven-year bull market, many investors find themselves owning individual securities with considerably higher dollar values than the recommended limit. When a portfolio is a victim of its own success, do some rebalancing. Sell some winners. This brings the individual security weighting back into equilibrium with the portfolio as a whole.

Selling securities can reduce tax

As the average Canadian spends more money annually on tax payments than on food and shelter combined. It is important to keep Revenue Canada with as small a piece of the action as possible. The timely selling of stocks can be an effective tax reduction strategy if the winners are sold in a year when the individual has a low tax rate. Selling losing positions and taking capital losses is also recommended when capital gains are high.

Since capital losses can be deducted against capital gains, this strategy can significantly reduce an investor's overall taxation.

It may be wiser to invest in better opportunities

Money does not grow on trees. Occasionally, the only way to take advantage of an exceptional investment opportunity is to sell an existing portfolio position with weak growth prospects. Then you can deploy the proceeds toward an investment that produces superior returns.

Reinvest in candidates that are cheap and out of favor

Stock price movement is driven by the tug-of-war between an investor's fear of loss and greed for gain. Fear and greed — irrational emotions — drive the price of stock. Classic investment strategy calls for buying companies when they are out of favor and low in price, and then selling them when investor enthusiasm pushes the share price above its fair market value. Overpriced stocks eventually lose investor interest and drop in price. Sell before this happens and reinvest the proceeds in candidates that are cheap and out of favor.

When a company is permanently having difficulty making profits, timely selling can maintain profits or at worst, cut losses. When a stock's attractiveness fades, its share price will decline in price to reflect its current financial prospects. Structurally impaired companies should be immediately sold and the money deployed to greener pastures.

The key to profits

Buying low and selling dear will keep your wallet full of cheer.
Wall Street

This proverb sums up what it takes to make money in the stock market. Profiting from equity investments requires becoming an expert in the art of buying — and selling.

A junior stock shopping guide

Junior stocks are in the start-up phase of their development. At this point in their corporate life, they are generally small, underfinanced and over-extended but... full of big ideas.

While the risks at this early stage are enormous, so are the rewards. Some juniors have demonstrated a 100 or even a 1,000-fold increase in value. Hot beds for this type of exponential growth can typically be found in the mining, oil, gas and high technology sectors of the economy.

Unfortunately, in high risk investing, a few smart people make most of the money. Due to a lack of information, misguided expectations and slick promotion, the rest become financial cannonfodder.

Correctly using the following check list can help tilt the odds of these high risk investments in your favor. In addition, it can help you separate fantasy from reality and point you towards investment candidates with suitable risk/reward profiles. Next time you are tempted to buy into a juicy investment story, subject it to the following 10-question check list. It's probably too high a risk if the junior company can't positively meet most of these criteria.

1. Does the product work? Is there proof? In the case of an energy or mining company, has sufficient drilling been done to verify substantial reserves?

Yes __ No __

2. Does the company have sales for the product it produces or manufacturers? Real money changing hands ultimately separates hype from reality.

Yes __ No __

3. Does the company make profits from the sales of its products? For shares to rise, a company has to make money. Ultimately, profits drive stock prices.

Yes __ No __

4. Are the company's sales and profits growing? The increase in a company's stock price parallels its growth in earnings. For example, companies that have profits growing at 20 percent per year will generally find their stock price progressing at the same rate.

Yes __ No __

5. Does the company have its debt under control? Unmanageable debt often leads a junior company to its financial grave.

Yes __ No __

6. Does the company have an experienced management team? If not, they will gain experience with your money.

Yes __ No __

7. Does management have a significant ownership stake in the company? If ownership is minimal or non-existent, their commitment and belief in the company's future is usually the same.

Yes __ No __

8. How many shares have been issued to investors? If the company has too many shares outstanding, then its profits will be too fragmented to be meaningful.

Yes __ No __

9. Are share prices low in relation to their future potential? If values are high, then all the good news is already built into the stock's current price.

Yes __ No __

10. Are the company's sales and profits sustainable over the long-term? If the company is a one-night wonder, its stock price will collapse with its sales.

Yes __ No __

Scoring. Total the yes responses.

Three or less: Better odds with Lotto 649.

Six or less: The fifth horse in the ninth race is probably a better bet.

Nine or 10: The company is a likely buy, for the speculative part of your portfolio.

When it comes to buying junior stocks, treat this list like an American Express Card — don't leave home without it.

How good are your trading skills?

As a rule, wealthy gamblers only make large bets when they know the odds are overwhelming in their favor. This also applies to investors who have successfully learned to profit from their activities in the stock market. To win at the investing game, you have to know what the odds are before you place the bet. This test will show you how savvy an investor you really are.

1. Of the 50,000 known kimberlite formations explored for diamonds, how many have ever developed into a commercial mine?
   a. 2,000 b. 500 c. 10 d. 50

2. What percentage of people who trade commodities make money?
   a. less than 3% b. less than 1% c. less than 10%
   d. less than 20%

3. What percentage of people who trade stocks lose money?
   a. 50% b. 25% c. 75% d. 85%

4. What percentage of properties that get staked for exploration ever become a producing metals mine?
   a. 10% b. 6% c. 1% d. 3%

5. After five years, how many start up companies are still in existence?
   a. 1 out of 5 b. 2 out of 5 c. 3 out of 5 d. 4 out of 5

6. What percentage of people who trade junior stocks lose money?
   a. 35% b. 95% c. 65% d. 80%

7. Over the '80s, the average US equity fund went up a total of 300 percent. How well did the average investor who traded in and out of an identical fund do, over the same period?
   a. 400% b. 200% c. 70% d. 30%

8. In a recent *Wall Street Journal* survey, what percentage of economists could accurately predict interest rate movements over a six-month period?
a. 15% b. 70% c. 50% d. 30%

9. What percentage of market timing newsletters actually beat the Dow Jones Industrial Average over a 10-year period?
a. 0% b. 7% c. 15% d. 30%

10. What percentage of analysts have been accurate to plus or - 10 percent in predicting the future earnings of a company?
a. 46% b. 62% c. 31% d. 82%

11. The average rate of return per year over the last 20 years from new stock market issues is:
a. 6% b. 12% c. -10% d. 3%

12. If you bought the Templeton Growth Fund each year with the same amount of money for 25 years, on the day the market was lowest, your return would be 18.3 percent. If you bought on the day the market was the highest, each year your annual return each year would be:
a. 3.4% b. 10.6% c. 17.5% d. 8.2%

13. The TSE averaged 12 percent per year between 1977 and 1995. Yet, if you were out of the market for the 10 best trading days during the period, your return would drop to:
a. 8.3% b. 5.7% c. 9.7% d. 11.1%

14. If two people invested money in stocks and each earned 12 percent per year for 20 years, the person who bought and held the portfolio would have how much more at the end of two decades than the person who traded the entire portfolio once a year? This difference takes into account the effects of taxes and standard buy and sell commissions of two percent.
a. 25% more b. 50% more c. 150% more d. 250% more

15. Gold has averaged what kind of return over the last 70 years?
a. 10% b. 15% c. -2% d. 4%

16. A recent US study of 200 mutual funds showed an annual return over five years of 12.5 percent. How much did the average mutual fund investor make over the same period?
a. 8% b. 12% c 6. -10% d. 2.2%

17. If you bought stocks and I bought risk free treasury bills on the day the stock market peaked during each of the last six bull markets, how long, on average, would it take your money to catch up in value to mine?
a. 7.5 years b. 10 years c. 1 year d. 3.5 years

18. After the market downturn of 1973, when did Disney and Coca Cola stocks get back to their 1973 highs?
a. 1975 b. 1980 c. 1986 d. 1991

19. John Doody's Gold Stock Analyst Index of North American gold stocks, which includes juniors as well as seniors, fell by what percentage between 1987 and 1998?
a. 25.1% b. 91.5% c. 60.7% d. 35.2%

20. The Dow Jones Industrial Average, on average, records a decline of 20 percent or more every:
a. 2 years b. 2.5 years c. 5 years d. 8 years

21. The Dow Jones Industrial Average, on average, shows a decline of 40 percent or more every:
a. 4.1 years b. 25.3 years c. 14.2 years d. 8.7 years

22. Between 1950 and 1996 the T.S.E. has averaged what type of return per year?
a. 15.3% b. 8.6% c. 10.7% d. 13.1%

23. For every 100,000 drugs that make it to phase one clinical trials, how many ever become a commercial success?
a. 32 b. 114 c. 216 d. 1

24. Over the last 200 years, what rate of real return has the US stock market been able to annually average?
a. 11.2% b. 14.7% c. 9.6% d. 6.9%

25. From January 1945 through December 1997 a portfolio of 100 percent US stocks would have averaged an annual compound return of 12.9 percent. A portfolio of 60 percent stocks and 40 percent bonds would have provided what annual compound return over the same period?
a. 6.2% b. 10.3% c. 8.6% d. 9.1%

26. The portfolio in the previous question that was 100 percent in stocks had a single worst year of - 26.5 percent since 1945. What was the single worst year over the same period for the portfolio that was 60 percent stocks and 40 percent bonds?

a. -14.9% b. -19.6% c. -11.73% d. -12.3%

27. Between 1939 and 1945, what investment would have lost you more money?

a. German bonds b. German stocks

28. Over the last 100 years, when has the US stock market shown the most volatility?

a. in times of war b. in times of peace

29. In 1979, the B.C. government did a study and found that investors buying stocks on the Vancouver Stock Exchange lost money what percent of the time?

a. 45% b. 69% c. 84% d. 96%

30. Over the last 30 years, Canadian stocks have had what type of performance compared to Canadian bonds?

a. better b. the same c. worse

31. Over any 20-year period since 1802, what percent of the time have US stocks outperformed US bonds and US treasury bills?

a. 70% b. 80% c. 90% d. 100%

32. 41 percent of all bond defaults come from what sector of the Canadian economy?

a. mining b. forestry c. technology d. real estate

33. What percentage of issued corporate bonds have defaulted since 1972?

a. 21% b. 3% c. 9% d. 14%

34. Studies show that ____ percent of family businesses make it to the second generation and ____ percent make it to the third.

a. 80% and 60% b. 90% and 50% c. 30% and 10%
d. 50% and 30%

35. Since 1886 the stock market on average declines in ____ out of every 10 years?

a. 4 b. 1 c. 2 d. 3

36. What percentage of day traders lose all their money within six moths?
a. 20% b. 90% c. 40% d. 70%

37. What percentage of restaurants fail or change hands in the first three years?
a. 90% b. 20% c. 60% d. 80%

This clearly shows that the odds of making money are overwhelming stacked against you when you engage in the following activities:

- trading mining and other speculative junior stocks;
- trading options or commodities;
- trying to time the market (when to get in and out);
- trying to predict earnings, interest rates, currency movements, etc.;
- indiscriminately buying new issues;
- trading stocks instead of holding them for the long-term;
- buying at market highs and not adding to positions when markets go down;
- buying gold for the purpose of building long-term wealth.

Indulging in any or all of the above high risk strategies can bring you closer to poverty.

Answers:

1.	d	11.	d	21.	d	31.	d
2.	a	12.	c	22.	c	32.	d
3.	c	13.	b	23.	d	33.	b
4.	c	14.	c	24.	d	34.	c
5.	a	15.	d	25.	b	35.	a
6.	b	16.	d	26.	a	36.	d
7.	c	17.	a	27.	a	37.	d
8.	d	18.	c	28.	b		
9.	b	19.	b	29.	c		
10.	a	20.	b	30.	b		

Widow and orphan stocks can help you make your $1 million

Would you rather have a BMW or a $1 million portfolio? If you're smart, you'll take that $50,000 (the cost of a new BMW) and invest it to create your portfolio. Here are some suggestions for choosing common stocks which produce uncommon returns.

The stocks that can help you make your $1 million portfolio are called widow and orphan stocks (W & O). The risk adverse can safely own stock in these sectors including banks, utilities, food processing, pipelines and other conservative industries. Since these stable companies produce essential products, they make substantial profits in good and bad markets. With large and consistent revenues, widow and orphan companies usually make substantial cash payments to shareholders (dividends) on a regular and increasing basis.

Performance hounds generally avoid widow and orphan stocks. However, buying blue chip stocks is the smartest path to a membership in the millionaire's club.

W & Os can be high performers

Here are some amazing sleepers:

Company	Business	10-year compounded return (percent)
Seagrams	Distillery	13
Bank of Montreal	Bank	13
B.C. Telecom	Telephone	14
Canadian Utilities	Gas utility	14
Pacific Northern Gas	Pipeline	17

These eye-popping returns will probably surprize you. Boring doesn't automatically equate to low performance. Following is a sampling of three model portfolios using widow and orphan stocks.

Income portfolio one

An investment of $50,000 in 1970, divided equally among the financial institutions of the Bank of Nova Scotia, the Bank of Montreal, the Royal Bank, the Toronto Dominion Bank and the Canadian Imperial Bank of Commerce would be worth about

$1,230,000 as of September, 1995. If all the dividends were reinvested into more shares of their respective companies over the 25-year period, the total rate of return on this portfolio would annualize at over 13 percent per year.

Income portfolio two

The *Investment Reporter*, a highly regarded Canadian market research publication, recently selected five stocks at random from their 1968 investment guide. These selections represented five different economic sectors: Bank of Montreal (financial); BCE Inc. (telecommunications); Thomson Corporation (publishing); B.C. Telecom (telecommunications); Imperial Oil (natural resources). Once again, if $10,000 was invested in each of these companies in 1968, they would be worth a total of $1,030.000 as of September, 1995. Over 27 years, with dividends reinvested and considering all stock splits, this portfolio would have grown at 11.41 percent per annum.

Income portfolio three

The third portfolio emphasizes international diversification. The list of US companies includes household names like McDonalds, General Electric, Proctor and Gamble, Merck and Walt Disney. If $10,000 Canadian had been placed in each of these US stocks on January 31, 1975, that portfolio would be worth $1 million on May 31, 1996. This group of higher performing stocks took about 21 years to reach $1 million because it returned 15.1 percent per year on an annual compound basis.

An equation for financial success at retirement

The equation for a healthy retirement income is very simple: wealth = time x dollars invested in widow and orphan stocks. With a consistent application of this formula your $50,000 today (or a BMW) could be a small fortune two decades from now.

A stock buyer's check list

Like most Canadians, you want to make money in the stock market, but don't want to risk the family farm. The following 12-point investment criteria will help you identify those companies that are long on opportunity but short on risk.

1. Buy companies where the insiders have been actively purchasing its shares. No one understands the future potential of a business better than its officers, directors and major shareholders. If a company's bankers are buying stock, that's even more encouraging. Lenders are risk adverse by nature, and normally will only invest when it looks like a sure thing.

2. Buy companies that are financially strong. Pay close attention to levels of debt. Be sure that the business has the ability to meet its fiscal obligations in good economic times as well as bad.

3. Buy companies that have a history of increasing their dividend pay outs. A growing dividend is proof a company can steadily increase earnings while affording to pay even bigger dividends. A weak company can't do both.

4. Buy companies that have dividend yields that are significantly higher than the market average. Today, average yields are 1.2 percent for stocks listed on New York Stock Exchange and 1.6 percent for those listed on the Toronto Stock Exchange. Companies offering cash payouts above the norm have historically shown returns superior to the market as a whole but with less volatility.

5. Buy companies where the share price is low in relation to the value of its assets per share. The essence of value investing is buying assets below their replacement cost.

6. Buy companies that have low price to earnings ratios (P.E.). P.E. ratios are valuable because they reveal how much an investor has to pay for each dollar of profits the company generates. Many investment pros will only buy stocks that have a P.E. ratio that's lower than its annual increase in profits. So for example, if a company is growing its profits at 15 percent per year, an investor wouldn't want to pay more than 15 times earnings for the shares.

7. Buy companies that have low price to sales ratios (P.S.). Price to sales or the P.S. ratio shows how much an investor has to pay per share for each dollar's worth of sales revenue that the company produces. A ratio of less than one is usually considered a bargain.

8. Buy companies that are monopolistic or are leaders in their field. Too many people selling the same product leads to cut throat pricing and low profitability.

9. Buy companies that benefit from essential services or habitual behavior. Businesses that profit from the regular buying habits of people produce sustainable earnings.

10. Buy companies whose earnings aren't tied to the business cycle. Sectors like resources, manufacturing and retailing have earnings that are overly dependent on the overall health of the economy.

11. Buy companies whose underlying business you understand.

12. Buy companies with Canada-wide (or even better, worldwide operations). The more geographic diversification a company has, the less its earnings will be affected by regional economic forces.

13. Buy companies with a strong management team and good labor relations. A business is only as good as the people who run it.

14. Buy companies that have had a recent pullback in share price. John Templeton had a rule that he would increase his holding in a company by the recent percentage drop in its share price. So if a corporation's share dropped in value by 30 percent, he would increase the amount of money he had invested in the company by 30 percent.

For every criteria your prospective stock meets, score one point. Companies that tally 12 points or more are suitable candidates for the conservative investor.

CHAPTER 10

PRECIOUS METALS

- All that glitters is not gold
- What's ahead for the shiny metal?

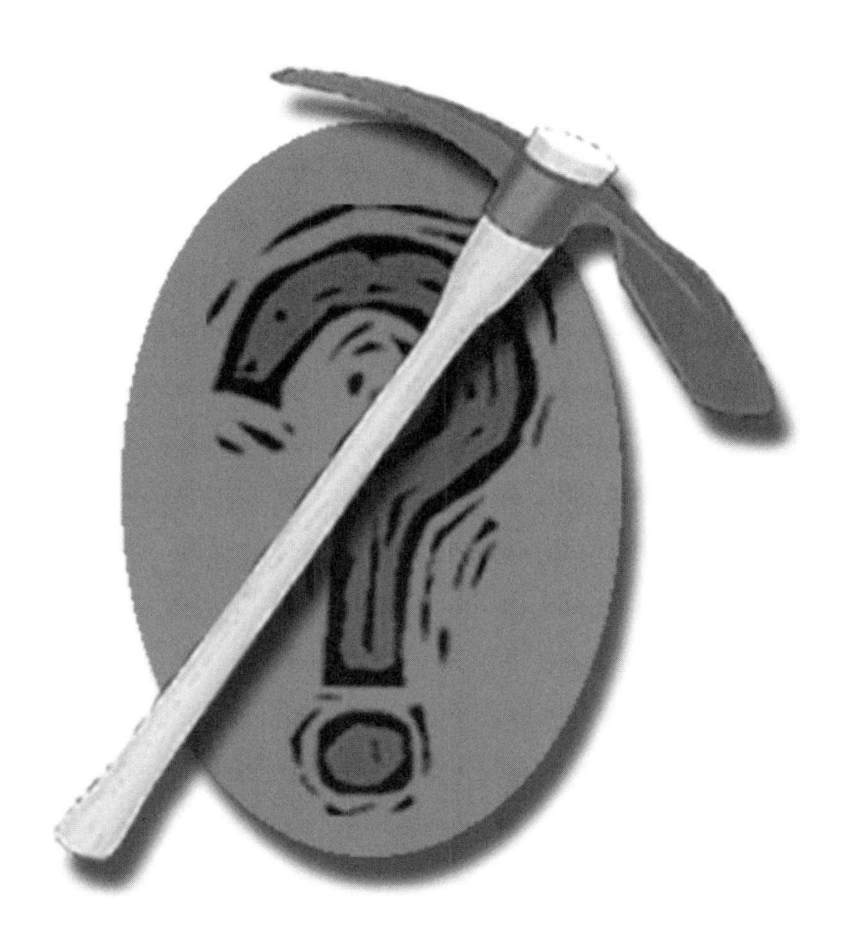

A study of economics usually reveals that the best time to buy anything is last year.

Marty Allen

A fool and his money are invited everywhere.

Anonymous

Advice is what we ask for when we already know the answer but wish we didn't.

Erica Jong

The broker you have, the broker you are.

Anonymous

All that glitters is not gold

To protect yourself against inflation or economic disaster, your best bet is gold, right? Hardly! During the inflationary cycle of 1970 - 1980, the myth of gold as a good investment gained favor. In that decade consumer prices doubled, and gold rose from $35 US per ounce to $850, an increase of 2,400 percent, or an average annual compounded rate of return of 37 percent. Considering this performance, it's no mystery why frightened money seekers see a lot of glitter in the yellow metal.

In reality, the long-term history of gold prices is tarnished. Dramatic movements of the yellow metal have been sparse. Over the last 200 years gold has made a major move three times: during the civil war; after the Arab oil embargo; during the hyper-inflationary late '70s and early '80s. Each of these three bull markets lasted only 3.7 years, on average. Added together, they produced only 10 profitable years for gold bugs. During the remaining 190 years, gold bugs spent much of their time in patient, profitless waiting.

Broad historical evidence shows that gold hasn't been a great long-term investment. Between 1781 and 1981, gold appreciated by a paltry 1.58 percent per year. Even isolating the heyday between 1926 and 1981, the increase was 5.77 percent annually. While this beat inflation and treasury bills (which both averaged three percent per year), it under performed the average stock on the New York Stock Exchange by four percent per year.

Another myth suggests that gold is the premier investment for inflation protection. Plotting its performance since 1910, gold hasn't out done any of its base metal cousins. If you wanted inflation insurance, brass, zinc or copper achieved the same investment performance. To hedge against inflation, a buy and hold strategy with a diversified portfolio of stocks would have served you much better than gold.

All these negatives don't necessarily make gold a bad investment. However, this suggests that investors in the precious metals haven't been successful in adopting a buy and hold strategy. As seen from the previous statistics, gold has made major gains in every 10 of the last 200 years or roughly about five percent of the time. To make money investing in gold, you have to TRADE IT. That is, buy and sell the metal to capture its profitable short-term swings.

Gold's short-term price fluctuations are explosive. Therefore, to effectively trade the metal, it is imperative to understand the factors triggering these swings such as inflation, disasters and supply and demand.

Inflation among the industrialized G7 countries is running about two percent, a long way from the 10 percent usually needed to drive gold prices. Unfortunately, the outlook for high levels of inflation is not overly optimistic, as reducing inflation is a priority for central bankers. However, if countries maintain large deficits, inflation will be higher, which could be very positive for gold prices. Wars, natural disasters, political upheavals and economic crises can hike the price of gold. Since they are unpredictable, an investor needs fast reflexes to profit from such events.

Overall, nothing is likely to ignite the price of gold over the near-term. Therefore, investors who are willing to wait for the yellow metal to glitter again, are going to have to be patient — very, very patient.

What's ahead for the shiny metal?

For gold bugs, 1999 was another gloomy year. Over the past 12 months the spot price of gold has plunged from $350 US per ounce to its current $300. This is another in a long string of disappointing years for the precious metal. In 1981, it reached an all-time high of $875 US per ounce. Despite its past history, many people believe that since gold has fallen so hard and stayed down so long, a turn-around is inevitable. Is this in the cards? Here is a review of the metal's current fundamentals.

Why the price of gold has been subdued

Demand has fallen below the level of supply. The world's central or government owned banks are huge holders of gold. These institutions have been selling gold in quantities that are too large for the current market to efficiently absorb. Because the supply is currently exceeding the demand, the price is weak. This trend is likely to continue as more countries sell their gold to pay down debt or to increase their foreign currency reserves.

Global inflation rates are at subdued levels. While gold thrives in periods of rapidly rising inflation, price levels in most industrialized countries are increasing at less than two percent per year. Even in third world nations where inflation was once epidemic, the curse seems to be broken. Countries like Brazil and

Argentina, that once boasted 100 percent annual inflation rates, are showing single digit cost of living numbers. With deflation more of a threat than inflation, it's unlikely that inflation will be a driver of gold prices any time soon.

The recent strength of the US dollar. Many people who once bought gold as a refuge against global calamity now hold the US dollar. This currency is portable and can be electronically wired to almost any destination on the planet. Dollars can be invested to earn interest, while gold collects dust. Since gold is priced in US dollars, it's now more expensive for buyers with other currencies to purchase bullion, thus further reducing demand and price.

What will cause the price of gold to rise?

Low prices will eventually squeeze supply. At today's gold prices, fully one-third of the world's mines have production costs that make operation uneconomic. As expected, many mines have closed, most notably Echo Bay's Lupin Mine. So far, only about 40 tons of annual capacity have been closed by North American firms, with another 25 tons of reductions coming from South Africa and maybe 10 tons from Australia. However, before gold hits bottom and starts to rally, at least 500 tons of high cost product has to be moth balled. It will take some time before supply is reduced to facilitate a significant rise in the price of gold.

Central banks will eventually quit selling reserves. About 20 years ago, almost two thirds of the world's gold was held by the globe's central banks. Today, due to large sales of the yellow metal, they only hold about one-third of the world's total. This percentage is expected to shrink even further as countries like Switzerland, Argentina, and Britain announce significant reductions of their gold reserves. Without central bank sales of gold, the demand for the metal would actually be greater than the current supply. Therefore, once central banks quit selling their excess reserves into the marketplace, the price of gold could rise significantly and explosively.

It will be a long wait for higher prices

While the economic forces are already in place to drop the supply of gold below the world's current demand, the wait has already been 16 long years. A close look at the fundamentals suggests that sustained higher prices are still aways off.

CHAPTER 11

BEATING THE TAXMAN

- Income splitting for tax savings
- Saving tax with a family loan
- When borrowing makes sense

The power to tax involves the power to destroy.
John Marshall

When everybody starts looking really smart, and not realizing that a lot of it was luck, I get scared.
Ralph Yavneh

A statistician is someone who can draw a straight line from an unwarranted assumption to a foregone conclusion.
Anonymous

Income splitting for tax savings

Next to being shot at and missed, nothing is really quite as satisfying as an income tax refund.
F.J. Raymond

With income splitting, you shift income from family members in a high tax bracket to those in a lower tax bracket. While a legitimate tax strategy, Revenue Canada's attribution rules make this strategy difficult to execute. The income directed to the lower taxed family member is taxed back into the hands of the higher income lender. Here are some practical ways to legally direct income into the hands of family members who pay less tax.

Take advantage of spousal RRSPs
The higher income earner should consider making contributions to a spouse's RRSP. Revenue Canada says that if the spousal contribution stays in the RRSP for at least three years, then it can later be withdrawn and taxed in the hands of the lower income spouse.

Ensure that the higher income earning spouse pays
Have the higher income spouse pay household expenses. The lower income spouse can then invest his or her earnings and pay lower tax on the profits. Since Canada Pension Plan benefits can be split among spouses, split this income with a lower income earning spouse.

Loan money to family members and pay them a salary
For individuals who own a business, pay a reasonable salary (what you would pay someone else to perform similar duties) to family members. Since these lower taxed family members have an earned income, they can contribute to their own RRSPs.

If one spouse lends money to another spouse to earn business income, that income will not be taxed into the hands of the spouse who lent the money.

Transfer capital to a lower tax bracket
Normally, if you lend money to your spouse to invest, the profits will be taxed back in your hands. However, if the spouse reinvests these profits, from that point on, any gains made on

those original profits will be taxed in the hands of the receiving spouse. The income produced on the original transfer will be taxed each year in the hands of the transferring spouse. This strategy transfers capital from a spouse in a high tax bracket to a spouse in a low tax bracket.

For example: Mr. Jones, in the top tax bracket, gives Mrs. Jones $100,000 to invest. Mrs. Jones invests the money and receives a 10 percent return each year for a 10-year period. After the ten years, Mrs. Jones has accumulated $159,375 of her own capital which is comprised of the $100,000 earned over 10 years on the original gift, plus $59,375 of income on income. This example assumes that Mr. Jones is paying the tax on the income earned each year on the original $100,000, but from that point on, the income is taxed in the hands of Mrs. Jones.

Lend or give money to adult children

Giving monetary gifts to children who are over the age of 18 can be done without any attribution back to the giver, with the understanding that once the money is given, it permanently belongs to the adult child. Neither the principal, nor any profits earned from it can have any conditions attached that requires them to be given back or shared with the parent at any future date.

Lending money to adult children, at low or no interest, results in the income being attributable back to the individual who lent the money for interest and dividends received and not for capital gains.

If a parent lends or gifts money to a minor, any profits made from investing that money are automatically taxed back into the hands of the parent with the highest income. Profits from capital gains are not taxed.

Income splitting puts more money in your pocket

Since the average Canadian family spends more money on taxes than on the combined costs of food, clothing and shelter, tax reduction strategies are critical. Income splitting is one of the last legal ways of beating the taxman.

Saving tax with a family loan

It used to be that high income individuals could reduce tax by lending money to family members who were in a lower tax bracket and then investing it in their name. This worked until Revenue Canada calculated the lost dollars of this income splitting exercise. Attribution rules were then introduced to plug this loop-hole. These rules block a high income earner from shifting assets to a low-income earner by attributing income earned on these investments back to the person who initially transferred the assets in the first place. You can legitimately avoid attribution rules, as long as other rules are followed.

Loans must be at the prescribed rates

To ensure that income earned from money lent to another family member doesn't get taxed in the hands of the lender, you must meet the following two conditions:

1. There must be a formal loan agreement that charges interest at Revenue Canada's prescribed rate;
2. The interest must be paid to the lender by January 30 of each following year.

Revenue Canada determines the prescribed interest rate

At the beginning of each quarter, Revenue Canada sets its prescribed rates that govern interest charges on these types of loans. This rate fluctuates. For the current three months ending September 30, 1999, the rate is five percent. This is one of the lowest prescribed rates since Revenue Canada started issuing them in 1984.

The prescribed rate stays for the life of the loan and doesn't change as Revenue Canada adjusts the prescribed rate from quarter to quarter. In other words, if you make a loan to a family member before the end of September, the interest rate charged on that loan can stay at five percent forever, regardless of how high the interest rate might rise in the future.

A real case scenario: Mr. and Mrs. Brown

For example, let's say that Mr. Brown, in the top marginal tax bracket, has $100,000 in cash. Mrs. Brown, on the other hand, has no income and no investible assets. Mr. Brown wants to invest in a bond to earn seven percent. Instead of investing the money in his name, Mr. Brown loans the money to Mrs. Brown using a formal loan agreement, with Revenue Canada's five percent interest rate charge. Mrs. Brown then takes the money and invests it in her name in the same bond paying the same percent.

Mrs. Brown gains $7,000 in revenue off the bond in the first year, yet pays no income tax. She has her personal exemption and a tax deduction for the $5,000 in interest that she had paid on the loan from Mr. Brown. Mr. Brown must include the $5,000 in his income for that year and pay tax on that amount.

If Mr. Brown bought the bond himself, he would have paid about $3,220 in tax on the $7,000 of income that the bond would have produced that year. This is assuming a top marginal tax rate in Alberta of approximately 46 percent. Instead, Mrs. Brown will end up paying no tax and he will end up paying a tax of $2,300 on the $5,000 worth of interest income that he had earned on the loan to his wife. This is an annual tax saving of $980.

Talk to your tax advisor regarding this strategy. You may have to move quickly to take advantage of the five percent rate, effective until September 30, 1999. If Revenue Canada sets a higher rate next quarter, this strategy will still be applicable, but not as advantageous.

When borrowing makes sense

Considering today's low interest rates and good stock market returns, there is a growing interest in borrowing money to invest. Here is a review of the risks and rewards of borrowing investment funds along with the maze of tax rules regarding deductibility of interest costs. While the rules can be complicated and stringent, sometimes it's advantageous to borrow money for investment purposes.

When is the debt good or bad?

Since you cannot deduct the borrowing costs to buy a house for your residence, raw land, consumer items, or an RRSP contribution, these items are considered bad uses of credit.

Borrowing to buy stocks, bonds, preferred shares, mutual funds, rental properties or a business will generally allow you to deduct the interest costs of your loan, with certain restrictions. With interest bearing investments, borrowing costs are deductible only up to the rate yielded by the security purchased. For example, if you borrowed funds at six percent to purchase a bond that pays four percent, you can only deduct four percent against the interest of the loan. Interest costs incurred to purchase preferred shares are deductible at 1.25 times the rate of the preferred share dividend. For example, if the preferred share dividend was four percent, interest could be deductible up to five percent.

An interest payment's deductibility depends on the use of borrowed funds. When the funds have been used for investment or business purposes, the funds are usually deductible. The investments must be expected to produce an income. If you use the borrowed funds to purchase commodities, futures or raw land, the interest payments aren't deductible. In purchasing common stock with borrowed money, the interest is generally deductible regardless of dividends received, provided the common shares have the potential to produce dividends in the future.

The exception to this rule is interest payments on funds borrowed to make an RRSP contribution. The government disallowed this practice in 1981.

How to create tax deductible debt

Some investment strategies involving borrowed money are worth considering. When a fully paid for home is re-mortgaged (and the proceeds are used for investment purposes), the interest payments are tax deductible.

You can also transform non-deductible interest into deductible interest. Use available cash to pay down personal loans and then borrow for investment or business purposes. As well, if you are simultaneously holding a portfolio of paid for securities and at the same time have non-deductible debt like credit cards, you may want to liquidate enough of your portfolio to pay off the non-deductible debt and then re-borrow to purchase more securities which make the interest on this new debt tax deductible.

Minimizing the amount of non-deductible debt you're carrying can be lucrative. For example, to match the return of paying down non-deductible debt with a 12 percent interest rate, you have to earn a 24 percent rate of return on a fully taxable investment.

If you don't have any non-deductible debt and don't want to involve your home, but would like to take advantage of deductible interest, consider using the margin capability offered by your broker. You borrow funds from your brokerage firm and use the securities purchased as collateral. You pay a percentage of cash for the investment (the percentage varies according to the type of security) and your brokerage firm lends you the rest.

Caveat emptor

With margin, you can enhance the profits on your own money. Leveraging also works the other way. Any losses incurred will be magnified and can exceed the original cash outlay. While borrowing money to invest isn't for everyone (it's more risky than paying cash), for active investors, it's an attractive way to accelerate an investment's profit potential.

A final warning. Discuss borrowing strategies with your financial and tax advisors. Because the rules are so complicated, it takes an expert to ensure that any of your borrowing meets the government's criteria for tax deductibility.

CHAPTER 12

PASSING THE TORCH TO THE NEXT GENERATION

- Are our kids worse off today?
- Survival strategies for Generation X
- Helping kids learn from the consequences
- New rules for RESPs

Buy a stock the way you would buy a house. Understand and like it such that you'd own it in the absence of any market.

Warren Buffet

We pay the debts of the last generation by issuing bonds payable by the next generation.

Lawrence J. Peter

Those who are of the opinion that money will do everything may very well be suspected to do everything for money.

Sir George Savile

Money makes money. And the money that money makes makes more money.

Benjamin Franklin

Are our kids worse off today?

Downsizing, wage stagnation and chronic unemployment are buzzwords of the '90s. Add offshore migration of manufacturing, workplace automation, global competition, huge national deficits and the relentless rise of taxation to the list of woes, and you'll be even more depressed. Not surprisingly, this constant bombardment of despair leaves many people thinking that life will never be as good for their children and grandchildren as it was for them. Despite the naysayer's gloom, many indicators suggest we have never been wealthier, a fact that makes your children better off than most of you think.

Expectations have changed

A US survey shows that 93 percent of those officially defined as being in poverty own a color television, and more than 60 percent have VCRs and microwaves. Applying today's standards to 30 or 40 years ago, families growing up in an average Edmonton or Calgary neighborhood would qualify for public assistance. Yet, at that time, these residents were considered middle class. When compared to some in our country, many Canadians feel poor. This comparison, however, is being made in a country with one of the world's highest standards of living.

Benefits have improved

Canada's public safety net protects citizens from mistakes that lead to abject poverty. Our medical coverage, employment, job retraining and social assistance programs are light years ahead of where they were 30 years ago. As a result, the taxes paid to receive these indirect benefits are also higher.

In 1965, benefits totaled about 25 percent of one's salary. Now, benefits between 40 and 50 percent of an employee's total compensation are common and include items like: paid vacations; pension plans; dental and medical insurance; disability compensation; paid maternity leave; education subsidies. The point is, while wages haven't risen much in recent years, total compensation has.

Workplace prejudices have changed

In the 1800s and 1900s, job opportunities were abundant for those with a strong back. Major employers wanted people who could sustain long hours of hard physical labor.

In today's job market the prejudices are different. Education is the bias. An average worker, with a high level of education, earns about $800,000 more salary over a lifetime than an uneducated worker.

The other prejudice is mobility. Skilled people who can move to countries with booming economies like the United States or Singapore will likely be swamped with job offers. Those who wait for the job to come to them, will be disappointed. In a changing workplace, individuals without an education and the ability to relocate will find the world equally as tough as those who lived 100 years ago.

The baby boomers will leave a legacy

It's estimated that the current generation of baby boomers will likely pass on about $2 trillion in wealth to their offspring. That capital will be used to buy houses, start businesses and pay off debt. This financial advantage is unparalleled in human history.

The distribution of work hours is different

Some people believe we are much worse off today because it takes two incomes to support a family, whereas a generation ago it took only one. The length of the work week can explain much of that difference. Even three decades ago, a single breadwinner often worked a 10-hour stint for at least six days a week. Today's typical work week is about 35 hours. A two-income family total is about 70 hours per week. The total work hours per week needed to support a family haven't really changed that much. The change is in how those hours are divided between family members.

Buying power has remained the same

About 30 years ago a starter home cost about three times a person's annual salary. A car was about equal to one year's salary. In today's job market, with an annual salary of $25,000, you can still buy a car for $25,000, and find a starter home for $75,000. Today's relative buying power is as good as it was 30 years ago.

Character is the most important asset

Your children face many challenges in today's economic environment. But is it tougher than it was a generation ago? I don't think so. If anything, this generation has more financial and educational resources than the previous one ever did.

As a parent or grandparent you need and want to help your children. However, it's important not to fall for the "things-are-so-bad" excuse. Unwisely, this leads to bailing your children out every time they get financially over their heads. If you get sucked into that argument, you reinforce the belief that the future is hopeless. Even worse, you will keep your children from learning that resourcefulness, hard work and perseverance are needed to overcome life's toughest challenges.

Survival strategies for Generation X

Thrift cannot be too highly commended. Teach all those with whom you come in contact to be saving. You never know when you may need their savings to finance one of your ventures.

Don Marguis

The 1990s will likely be remembered as the decade when large bureaucracies were dismantled. On any given day, in any type of media, headlines broadcast dreary stories about government and corporate downsizing, from the Soviet Union's collapse to the layoff of thousands of employees by the nation's industrial giants. Like ancient dinosaurs who cannot cope with fast change, these large organizations are on the endangered list.

For Generation X, the world will be completely unlike the one experienced by their parents and grandparents. Today, large paternal organizations and governments don't hire workers after graduation and employ them until retirement at age 65.

Rather, Generation X can expect many careers in a lifetime. Part-time and contract work is the norm. The large organization doesn't fuel the economic engine. Rather, small business runs the engine. Small companies, comprised of highly energetic entrepreneurial individuals, are set apart, not by ability, but by mind set. These men and women realize that in today's world, security is created by relying on your own skills and initiative.

Unfortunately, Generation X is deficient in financial and entrepreneurial skills. The problem probably starts with the older generation. Having experienced considerable hardship in the past, many older people vow that future generations will never have to experience the same thing. When financial needs and whims are provided by parents and grandparents, there is little incentive for young people to exercise financial management skills. Today's kids are generally unprepared for the future's enormous challenges. Here are some suggestions on helping your offspring develop solid financial and entrepreneurial skills.

Teach them how to be an entrepreneur

Help your children or grandchildren create financial opportunities. Encourage them to look for work in your community. Accompany them door-to-door. Ask the neighbors if anyone needs snow shovelled, lawns mowed or fences painted. This teaches the importance of seeking out economic opportunities — being your own boss — rather than working for someone else.

Teach them how to save

Accompany your children or grandchildren to a financial institution where they can open a savings account. Parents can encourage good saving habits by requiring children to save a certain percentage of their allowance or earnings from odd jobs and part-time work. With every deposit, update their passbook. Quickly, they'll see the power of compounding. They'll learn how to make their money work — how to make it grow.

Give gifts with lasting value

Toys are great gifts, but after a few years, they get broken, are lost, or are given away. To provide something of lasting value, give cash or investments like Canada Savings Bonds. These gifts can be used for post secondary education.

Teach the principle of ownership

Buy children shares in companies on their level. Stocks represent the ownership of business. As a part-owner, they will come to understand the link between the ethereal world of investing and the real world. In being a part of successful companies like McDonald's and Disney, young people can own something they can feel, see and taste.

When you purchase a stock in your child's name (i.e. Sarah) have the certificate delivered to her. This makes the process of ownership more real. Show Sarah the annual report when it arrives. Teach her how to find the company's share price in the newspaper. When dividend cheques come in the mail, further explain about the additional rewards of owning a profitable company. Most importantly, show her the long-term history of the company and explain how much her money would have grown by holding the stock for an extended period of time.

Help children set goals

Children need to have personal financial goals such as saving for skis or a new bicycle. Help Bruce break a goal into achievable pieces. Show him, week by week, or month by month, how much he needs to save to reach his target. In the process, you will instill the important lesson that rewards come with discipline and sacrifice.

Your children's future depends on you

Children will only develop adequate financial skills if you teach them. Not only will your personal involvement put them at an advantage, you'll have a chance to practice what you preach.

Helping kids learn from the consequences

Estimates suggest that over the next 20 years the current crop of Canadian baby boomers will pass on $1.5 trillion dollars to their children and grandchildren. This will be the largest intergenerational transfer of wealth in Canada's history.

While prosperous parents and grandparents want to help their offspring financially, they also don't want to deprive them of learning how to stand on their own two feet. Here are some reasons why children should be allowed to learn needed lessons.

The pitfalls of unearned wealth

What an individual is, not what he or she has, is the true essence. For many young people, the unearned and undeserved arrival of large sums of money can easily smother initiative. When too much is given too soon, an individual doesn't learn important life skills like determination, perseverance, hard work and goal setting.

Success is built upon the foundation of past mistakes and failures. We often learn more from errors than victories. Failure teaches permanent lessons. When parents bail their kids out monetarily every time they make a mistake, kids don't learn the important lessons, and they don't grow and change in response to that situation.

Don't repeatedly bail out your offspring

Emotion is often a big stumbling block to reining the purse strings to kids and grandkids. Many people can feel very guilty watching offspring struggle, while they enjoy the financial fruit of many years of labor. The mind has to make a huge emotional leap to enjoy a Caribbean cruise, while your kids sweat to make the monthly mortgage payment. For many, the guilt would be so overwhelming that they couldn't enjoy a cruise, even if they went.

For most kids or grandkids, things aren't as difficult as when their parents and grandparents were starting out. Back then, a social safety net wasn't even in existence. Despite the rhetoric, times are easier and we are wealthier then we've ever been.

Older adults grew up and flourished in a world that was far less supportive than the one young people now enjoy. Perhaps this realization may make it easier to resist the temptation to bail out offspring.

Give help, with strings attached

The best way to help children is to instill values and teach responsibility. Get them to do their part. No free lunches. No something for nothing arrangements. For example, if an adult child is saving for a down payment on a home, tell him or her to save a portion and you'll kick in the remainder. If you're helping a son or daughter go to school, let him or her pay off the cost of tuition and books. You'll reimburse them and reward responsibility with a passing grade. Have a son or daughter pay something for taking over your business. If necessary, defer payment until the business is successful.

Life is cause and effect. If you do things right, you reap the rewards. If you err, you suffer the effects. The best way to help children financially is to let them learn from the consequences of their actions.

New rules for RESPs

New rules in the Federal budget make RESP (Registered Educational Savings Plan) very attractive. However, the volume of regulations on the subject confuse almost everyone. In a straight-forward Q & A format, here are answers to the most commonly asked questions about RESPs.

Q: Are contributions to an RESP tax deductible?

A: Unlike RRSPs, investors don't get an up front tax deduction when they contribute to a Registered Educational Savings Plan. However, like an RRSP, any growth made on investments inside of the plan are tax sheltered for the time they remain in the plan. When the money is taken out of an RESP plan, it's taxed in the hands of the beneficiary of the plan as long as that person is using the money to go to an approved institution of higher learning (beyond high school).

Q: How much money can be contributed toward the plan of any single beneficiary?

A: The maximum that can be contributed in any given year to any beneficiary is $4,000. The overall lifetime limit is $42,000 worth of RESP contributions per child.

Q: Who can contribute to an RESP plan?

A: Anyone can contribute to an RESP plan, as long as they're related to the beneficiary of the plan (the person who is actually going to use the money to go to school) by blood or adoption.

Q: What is the lifespan of an RESP plan?

A: An RESP must be terminated at the end of the 25th year of the plan. Contributions to a particular plan may be made for up to 22 years.

Q: If I can't contribute the full $4,000 per child in any given year is the amount lost?

A: No. The amount can be carried forward and used in future years.

Q: What is the Canadian Educational Savings Grant?

A: The government will give a 20 percent grant for every dollar that's put into an RESP up to a maximum of $2,000 per year. If a person puts $2,000 into an RESP for their child this year, the government would contribute $400. A carry-forward provision allows you to skip years and catch up on missed grants. Since grants are not payable to children age 18 or over, the maximum amount of grant that any child can accumulate is $7,200 ($400 x 18 years).

Q: Does my child need anything else to qualify for this grant?

A: RESPs can be set up without a social insurance number for the child, but grants will only be paid out when the child's SIN number has been provided to the government.

Q: What happens to the grant if my child opts for other than four full years of university (or equivalents as set out in the RESP contract)?
A: You must repay the original grant the government gave you, but you can keep the income generated by the grant money.

Q: What happens to my contributions and the growth on them if my child doesn't choose to go on to a higher education?
A: With any RESP, the parents will get their original invested capital back if the child doesn't go. Other options include:

- transferring the beneficiary to another child who is pursuing higher education;
- parents taking out the growth portion of the plan and getting taxed on it at their top rate plus an additional 20 percent penalty;
- transferring the money to an RRSP. In this case, growth on the RESP plan can be transferred to the parent's RRSP plan to a maximum of $40,000. This has been increased to $50,000 in 1999. This option will only work if there is contribution room in their RRSP to take a $40,000 addition.

Q: What kinds of investments can I make with an RESP?
A: That depends on the plan. With self-directed plans you can invest in a wide variety of stocks, bonds and mutual funds. In a plan offered by a mutual fund company you choose within their family of funds. Pooled RESP products are generally limited to government guaranteed fixed income investments.

Before investing in any RESP plan read the fine print of the prospectus. The devil is always in the details. The new rules for RESPs have plenty of those.

CHAPTER 13

INVESTING OFFSHORE

- Why go offshore?
- Offshore investment structures
- Is a tax haven practical?

You try to be greedy when others are fearful and fearful when others are greedy.

Warren Buffet

The worst mistake investors make is taking their profits too soon and their losses too long.

Michael Price

When I have to depend upon hope in a trade, I get out of it.

Jesse Livermore

The only person wise about the future is the person who keeps silent.

John Kenneth

Why go offshore?

In recent years, tax havens have become incredibly popular by those seeking refuge from high taxation, increasing levels of litigation and government's growing intrusion into people's private lives. Ken Finkelstein, author of *The Tax Haven Guide Book*, estimates that over 50 percent of the worldwide money supply is parked offshore among the world's 50 tax havens. In 1997 alone, he says that almost 50,000 new corporate registrations were made offshore. This chapter looks at the advantages and disadvantages of tax havens, the types of investment structures available and what different havens offer in the way of services.

Reasons for investing offshore

The most common reasons to park money in a tax haven include:

- financial privacy;
- tax savings;
- litigation and asset protection;
- retirement/lifestyle;
- protection from governments.

Privacy

Most offshore jurisdictions have strict secrecy laws which enshrine a person's right to financial privacy. Reducing one's financial profile can be especially useful in discouraging frivolous litigation, fraud, theft or simply keeping sensitive information away from the prying eyes of governments, neighbors or competitors.

With a view of making foreign investments more transparent, foreign income verification rules have been in place since April,1997. Revenue Canada says that individuals with an interest in a foreign affiliate or who have more than $100,000 invested outside of Canada must report this information.

Tax savings

Since 1961, the consumer price index has risen by 450 percent, yet taxation has skyrocketed by 1200 percent over the same period. Canadians live in one of the highest taxed and highest debt-ridden countries in the world. Not surprisingly, places that levy no personal income tax and protect investor's privacy are attractive.

Many people have the misconception that money can be earned offshore and as long as it stays there and is not brought back into the country where you are a taxpayer, it remains tax free. Revenue Canada thinks otherwise. Through rules like Foreign Accrual Property Income (FAPI), Bill C-92, with its offshore disclosure rules, and GAAR (General Anti-Avoidance Rules) they have an arsenal of legislation designed to close most of the tax advantages associated with offshore investing.

Revenue Canada says they have the right to know where the taxpayer's money is located and how it's invested so they can determine how much tax should be levied on the income from any particular scheme. According to them, you are obliged to report any income, gain or dividend, regardless of where that money was earned and pay tax on that amount.

Experts suggest that tax free structures can still be created. However, understanding the intricate details of these plans requires greater ingenuity and access to very sophisticated advice. Since Revenue Canada is continually modifying its rules to close these structures, individuals involved in tax havens must constantly be scrutinizing and fine tuning these structures to stay ahead of the taxman.

Asset protection

With the cost and amount of litigation increasing each year, asset protection is a priority. When properly established, offshore structures can shield assets from lawsuits, creditors, divorce or even bankruptcy. Doctors, dentists, engineers, accountants and business owners, at a higher risk for malpractice suits, find asset protection trusts appealing. Since there is no tax advantages in investing offshore, asset protection tends to be the most popular choice for legitimately moving money out of the country.

Lifestyle and retirement

Many Canadians leave the country to work or retire in a warmer climate. As we are taxed based on our residency, this can have big financial advantages. Since non-residents don't have to pay Canadian tax on their world income, a valid tax planning tool is to live outside Canada for more than 183 days per year.

To prove that non-residency status is permanent, a person is required to severe most of their ties to the country which means selling a principal residence, closing bank accounts, etc.

At the time a person declares non-residency, Revenue Canada requires that fair market value be attached to the person's assets and tax be paid on all assets at the time of emigration. RRSPs have special rules which allow them to be collapsed with a tax penalty of only 25 percent.

Many people like the idea of becoming a non-resident so they can move to a jurisdiction where they pay no income tax. Usually, they find that the tax savings compensates for the higher cost of living and the extra expense of additional health care insurance.

Protection from governments
Most western nations irresponsibly manage their fiscal affairs. History has shown that nothing reduces prosperity faster than high taxes, high debts and high deficits. People concerned about the long-term destruction of wealth accompanying these policies often opt for the safety of an offshore account.

Offshore investment structures

An investor faces two challenges in investing offshore:

1. Getting money out of Canada;
2. Picking a suitable investment vehicle.

Here is a review of the most commonly used structures to house investments offshore.

The International Business Company (IBC)
An offshore corporation is usually established to hold bank accounts, credit cards, purchase goods and services, hold property or trade securities. It can conduct any financial transaction in its own name while hiding the real identity of its owner. Canadians who set up an International Business Company generally use them to invest in securities like stocks, bonds or mutual funds or to hold real estate. On average, the cost of setting up an IBC is about $2,000. Maintenance and registration fees can cost another $1,000 per year.

The offshore bank account
Offshore accounts can be established in the name of an individual, trust or corporation. Setting up such an account is as easy as opening an account at your local bank. In most cases, you don't have to visit the offshore bank in person as the documents can be delivered to your home.

Since they normally pay no income tax and deal with sophisticated clientele who want more options, offshore banks usually offer more services than domestic ones. These institutions generally deliver a far broader range of investments, have international trading facilities and research, offer choices on deposit accounts denominated in most major currencies and have much higher rates of interest on deposit accounts.

The offshore investment account

While this account can be opened to trade individual securities, the most popular choice is for investment funds offered by offshore banks, trust and mutual fund companies. Income generated from these funds is normally rolled back into the fund and is not taxed. Accounts owning offshore funds are generally held in the name of the financial institution administrating them to guard the investor's anonymity.

Besides their deferred taxation, another advantage of offshore funds is their management fees. They are typically half of those paid for a domestic mutual fund. *Standard and Poor's Micropal Guide to Offshore Investment Funds* is a good source of information on offshore funds. It surveys more than 6,800 of the more than 14,000 offshore funds and gives detailed information on the top 350.

Offshore trusts

A trust is an arrangement where property or assets from one person (usually the one that owns the asset) are transferred to another (usually an offshore trustee such as a bank, trust or established law firm). This enables that investor, on the surface, to divest themselves of assets like stock, cash, real estate or company shares and cloud the question of ownership. The assets are registered in the name of the trustee who has an obligation to manage them according to precise terms set out by the owner in a document called a trust deed. This allows the investor to run the show and get the trustee to do his or her bidding.

A trust is not registered with any government agency and the identities of the interested parties are protected by the tax haven's secrecy laws.

Setup costs for a trust can run between $4,000 and $7,500 and $2,000 to $4,000 a year for maintenance.

A word of caution

Many offshore structures involve transferring assets into another's name to insure anonymity. To do this, you must trust this person. Do your homework and make sure you are working with honest and reputable people.

To achieve the highest level of security, stick with big international financial institutions like Credit Suisse, ABN Ambro, UBS, Hong Kong Shanghai Bank, Barclays Bank, Ing,

Citibank, Deutsche Bank, Royal Bank of Scotland, Chase Manhatten or the Bank of Bermuda, just to name a few. These offshore banks have a history of:

- financial strength;
- stable management and ownership;
- growth;
- adherence to secrecy.

While dealing with reputable financial institutions can cost a little more, the additional security is worth your peace of mind. A mom and pop operation, and your money, can fold tomorrow.

Is a tax haven practical?

Currently, over 50 countries are considered to be tax havens. Anguilla is small. Others, like the Cayman Islands, have over $550 billion domiciled on its shores, making it, after New York, Tokyo and London, the fourth biggest financial center on the planet.

Whatever tax haven you choose, consider some practical issues like language, communications, location, political stability and taxation.

Language

If English is your spoken language, bank in a country where this is the official language. If not, you'll have to expend extra time and money for translation. Having your instructions misunderstood can be risky and expensive.

Communications

The country should have at least one major airline connection, a daily postal service and a good telecommunications infrastructure that can be quickly accessed by phone, fax or e-mail. Fast, reliable service is essential if you are trading securities or need to execute timely business decisions.

Location

Many people want a location that's easy to get to. Also consider time zones. For an Albertan dealing with a bank in the Turks and Caicos, the difference is two hours. It's a 20-hour difference if you're dealing with a financial institution in the Cook Islands.

Political stability

Don't even consider countries with political unrest. Be especially wary of dictatorial regimes and states that have recently embarked on a road towards democracy. Your money gets lost when these countries follow a pattern of taking two steps forward and one step back.

Bank secrecy laws

It's preferable to invest in a haven that has passed and enforces laws covering bank secrecy.

Professional services

Tax havens vary dramatically in the availability and quality of professional services offered. If you have sophisticated requirements, avoid less developed countries.

Multiplicity

Authorities in both Canada and the US have, on several occasions, successfully defeated the confidentiality laws of certain tax havens to obtain information about a resident of their own country. In many cases, a multi-jurisdictional approach would have solved this problem as it suggests that no single country would have all the information to give an interested third party should confidentiality become threatened.

Specific expertise

Amidst heated competition, many offshore centers have specialized. The Cook Islands, Caymans, Turks, Caicos, Cyprus, Gibraltar and Bahamas focus on asset protection. Switzerland, Jersey, Guernsey and the Caymans specialize in asset management. Services for incorporation are excellent in the Bahamas, British Virgin Islands and Panama. The Isle of Mann is renowned for its insurance expertise. Barbados, Caymans, Turks and Isle of Mann have also established a speciality in limited liability companies. To determine the most appropriate tax haven, consider the expertise you need.

Costs

Bermuda, the Cayman Islands and Switzerland are among the most expensive places to invest, although they have superior banking, government supervision and access to professional services. Panama, Costa Rica and Belize are cheaper, but lack quality services. With offshore investing, quality doesn't come cheap.

Taxation

While some havens have no direct taxation, others like Barbados have corporate tax rates of 2.5 percent. Bermuda only grants incorporation rights to those with the most impressive credentials. Most of us aren't welcome in that country. If granted incorporation, you are exempt from tax for 20 years, and are not allowed to compete against local business. In Ireland you are not taxed on your world income, but are taxed on domestic profits.

Since each haven has a myriad of tax rules and regulations, picking an appropriate jurisdiction is not a job for an amateur. Have a professional, who understands and specializes in tax havens, review your situation. The extra dollars are a small price to ensure your financial future.

Recommended reading:

The Tax Haven Guide
by K. Finkelstein

The Sovereign Individual
by J. Davidson

Offshore Advantage
by G. Laight

S & P Micropal Guide to Offshore Investment Funds
by R. Milroy

ABOUT THE AUTHOR

Ron Hiebert

Ron Hiebert is one of Alberta's leading wealth building, personal finance, retirement and estate planning experts. An accomplished speaker, author and financial advisor, Albertans know and trust Ron for his "tell-it-like-it-is" approach to financial planning.

Ron is an associate director at ScotiaMcLeod and has been with the firm since 1983. He currently manages over $180 million for both local and international clients. Ron specializes in providing integrated personal investment, retirement and estate planning advice. A popular financial speaker and author, he is recognized for his ability to provide practical, up-to-date advice.

Ron hosts *Making Money*, the popular Sunday morning financial talk show on CHQT 880 radio. He also gives daily stock market commentaries on CHQT. Media such as CBC (radio and television) and CFRN (radio and television) frequently ask for his financial analysis on a wide range of topics. Ron is on the advisory board of *Today's Choices*, Alberta's only magazine for living even better after 45, and contributes a monthly financial column to the magazine. He also writes a weekly financial tip for the *Edmonton Sun*.

In 1993, Ron co-authored *Making Money the Old Fashioned Way*, an easy-to-read, easy-to-follow book on basic investing.

Ron has an M.Sc., from California State University, is a Fellow of the Canadian Securities Institute and holds a C.I.M. (Canadian Investment Manager) designation. In 1991, he won the investment community's **Distinction Award** for the province of Alberta. Ron teaches an investment course through the Faculty of Business at the University of Alberta.

Ron lives in St. Albert, and is happily married with four children. Away from the stocks, bonds and mutual funds that make up a usual day at ScotiaMcLeod, Ron enjoys fly fishing, water sports, traveling and camping.

MAKING MONEY FOR THE RIGHT REASONS

Ron and Silver

In November 1996, Ron Hiebert was featured in *Today's Choices* magazine. That article is reprinted below. In the article, written by Elsie Rose, editor, *Today's Choices*, Ron talks about his approach to investing.

Most of us are familiar with the enthusiastic voice that offers financial advice on CHQT 880 every Sunday morning on *Making Money* (from 10 a.m. to 11 a.m.) and throughout the weekday on *Market Update*. Ron Hiebert is Alberta's home-grown, highly respected and greatly admired financial wizard. But he's also one heck of a nice guy.

Most of us may not recognize this down-to-earth, tell-it-like-it-is financial advisor decked out in hip-waders fly-fishing for trout on the Adams River, in jeans and baseball cap paddling down the

Colorado River, or screaming with delight in a Formula Ford at the Skip Barber Driving School in Hawaii.

Away from the stocks, bonds and mutual funds that make up a usual 7:30 a.m. to 6:30 p.m. day at ScotiaMcLeod, Ron Hiebert lives what he preaches. For Ron, life (and money) is really about living. Even more so, it's about being grateful for friends and family — those things that matter most to him.

"Money is about time and energy," says Ron. "The amount you save reflects your ability to defer present gratification for future rewards. Money tells you a lot about people, as it often reflects their view of life."

Ron says it is important to find out what that view is. "Financial independence is about the kind of life you want to have. While money can't buy you happiness, it can buy you freedom and choices. That freedom means different things to different people. Cruises, travel and a new car every two years take more money than reading by a fireplace."

Reaching financial independence requires large doses of reality. "Most people invest with a rear view. They are moved by what other people are doing. In 1984 people were line-up around the block to buy gold at its record high of $800 an ounce. They arrived when the party was over.

"The last few years, people have been buying mutual funds as if they were the ticket to riches. I'm not saying you shouldn't buy mutual funds, but you have to separate the hype from reality. Out of thousands of mutual funds, only four have produced consistent annual returns of 15 percent over a 10-year period. The average is less than eight percent over 10 years.

"Media hype says you need $1 million to retire. But if you talk to "real" people, who have been retired for many years, you'll find they are doing just fine on $30,000 to $40,000 a year. You have to screen out the vested interests, and the smoke and mirrors the financial industry has created for itself. Financial decisions are often made on fear, hope and emotion."

Ron calls this — a balanced, realistic perspective of financial independence — the art of *Making Money*. He passes on his philosophy in a monthly column of the same name in the magazine *Today's Choices*, his first book *Making Money the Old Fashioned Way*, and his Sunday morning financial show on CHQT.

For his first book, Ron interviewed some 1,000 people to find the secrets of financial independence. "I regularly go to lunch with my clients, people I respect and admire. They continually tell me the realities of building wealth, and I see from their example that making money is not that difficult."

Ron, who holds degrees in communications and administration, and who holds numerous financial designations, sums up the road to financial independence from those who are already there:

- get out of debt;
- live within your means;
- set up a systematic savings plan in something you understand.

Ron says a critical point is age 40-45. "If you are debt-free, then you can start a regular savings plan. You can retire, comfortably, with time, compounding and cash flow. Financial independence has little to do with education or income."

On the other hand, Ron says that a 60-year-old with a 10-year mortgage has fewer choices. "You'll likely have to drastically restructure, continue working, change your lifestyle or downsize."

Ron says retirement planning is about working backwards. "You have to ask the question, 'What is it going to take for me to be happy, in dollars and cents terms?' Then you develop a financial plan to reach those goals."

As Ron looks back on his 14-plus years in the business and his choices made, he has no regrets. "I'm not going through the classic crisis some people have at midlife. I've done all the adventurous things I've wanted to do. A few years ago, I look a sailing course. I'm taking voice lessons now. A few years ago I went scuba diving for a week on the Great Barrier Reef.

"As for the future, that includes bike trips and backpacking with my family, building an airplane with my wife, Penny, and who knows what else. There is a whole world of things out there to do. This adds spice and flavor, and that makes life marvelous. I have no plans to stop. When my time is up, I hope it's paddling down a waterfall."

GLOSSARY OF TERMS

Equity funds Risk
PENNY
Taxation
OPTION STOCKS
Coupon
Earned income
Gambling
Load
New issue
Liquidity
Down Jones Industrial Average
Marketability
OFFER Junk
Leverage
bond
ADR Net worth
Margin

ACCOUNTANT: A person who organizes financial information.

ACCRUED INTEREST: The accumulated interest on a loan.

ACTUARIES: Professional odds-makers who study life expectancy or mortality rates for insurance purposes.

ACTUARY TABLES: Documents produced by actuaries which forecast average life expectancy for men and women.

ADR: An abbreviation for American Depository Receipt. Refers to some foreign shares trading on a US stock exchange.

AFTER-TAX COST: The final cost of an investment to an investor in a particular tax bracket, after calculating the effect of income tax.

AGGRESSIVE INVESTMENT: An investment concerned primarily with capital growth rather than income or security.

ALL-OR-NONE: This order prevents a broker from filling an order in bits and pieces, which could lead to higher commissions because of a minimum cost for each transaction. An ALL-OR-NONE transaction must be for the exact number of shares specified.

ANNUAL REPORT: A statement of results issued by a company to its shareholders at the end of the fiscal year (the company's year-end) containing reports on company operations and formal audited financial statements.

ANNUITY: An investment that returns the principal and interest in a series of regular payments.

AMORTIZATION PERIOD: The time period it takes before a loan is completely repaid.

ASK (OFFER): The price at which a seller offers his/her security or property for sale.

ASSETS: An item you own. Any item, whether tangible or intangible, that is expected to provide future benefits. These benefits include income and capital growth.

ASSET ALLOCATION: The planned percentage distribution of your investment assets into various categories such as bonds, preferred shares, mutual funds, common shares, precious metals and real estate.

ASSET VALUE: The monetary value of holdings; sometimes expressed as asset value per share by dividing a total asset figure by the number of shares outstanding.

AVERAGE DOWN: Buying more of a security at a lower price than the original investment. The aim is to reduce the average cost per unit.

AVERAGE UP: To buy more of an investment after it has risen in price in an effort to capture more gain.

BACK-END LOADED MUTUAL FUND (BACK-END REDEMPTION CHARGE): A mutual fund where the sales commission is paid at the time of selling the fund.

BALANCED FUND: A mutual fund that invests in both interest bearing securities such as bonds and mortgages and equity investments such as preferred and common shares.

BALANCE SHEET: One of the financial statements that shows the financial position of an individual or company at a specific point in time. It is a record of assets, liabilities and shareholders' equity at that time. It is based on the equation: Assets = liabilities + shareholders' equity.

BANK RATE: The minimum rate at which The Bank of Canada makes short-term advances to the chartered banks and other deposit-taking institutions.

BASIS POINT: One basis point is one one-hundredth of a percentage point and is used to express bond yields. Thus, the difference between six percent and seven percent is 100 basis points.

BEAR MARKET: A market where prices are falling.

BID: The price at which an investor is willing to buy a particular stock or bond.

BLUE CHIP STOCK/COMPANY: A term describing a large, high quality company. Shares issued by large, well-financed, profitable, and established companies.

BLOCK: A significantly large number of shares of stock or other securities.

BOARDLOT: A unit of trading, which for most stocks is usually 100 shares if the stock trades above $1.

BOOK VALUE OF COMMON SHARES: The total assets of an enterprise minus intangible assets, liabilities, and preferred stock, divided by the number of outstanding common shares.

BONDS: IOUs with a set interest rate, backed by collateral, issued by governments and corporations and repaid over a fixed period.

BOND FUND: A mutual fund that invests in a widely diversified portfolio of bonds with different maturities. A bond fund normally includes bonds issues by the three levels of government as well as by blue chip corporations.

BROKER: A financial intermediary who acts as an agent in the buying and selling of securities or commodities, on a commission basis.

BUDGET: A financial statement of estimated income and expenses for a future period of time. It is frequently used as a financial blueprint to summarize income, savings, and investment objectives.

BULL MARKET: A market where prices are rising.

CALL: An agreement under which a person may buy a certain quantity of stock or securities at a specified price for a specified time period.

CAPITAL GAIN (OR LOSS): The gain or loss that results from the sale of a capital asset. It is the difference between the original purchase cost and the sale proceeds.

CAPITALIZATION: A company's value is the multiple of its outstanding shares times the current market price. Companies are often classified as being small cap (up to $100 million), mid-cap ($100 million to $1 billion), large cap (over $1 billion).

CAVEAT EMPTOR: A Latin credo that means "Let the buyer beware."

CERTIFICATE OF DEPOSIT (CD): A time deposit with a specified maturity date.

CLOSE: The last price at which a security trades during a trading period.

CLOSED-END FUND: These are mutual funds where the units are bought and sold on the open market.

COLLATERAL: Assets promised by a borrower to a lender in case a loan cannot be paid back.

COMMISSION: The broker's or agent's fee for buying or selling securities for a client.

COMMON SHARE: Basic unit of ownership in a company.

COMPANY: An entity created for the purpose of carrying on a business.

COMPOUND INTEREST: The process of adding interest payments on to the original loaned amount as the payments come due, thereby creating a larger loan amount on which more interest can be earned.

CONVERTIBLE BOND/DEBENTURE: A bond or debenture that can be exchanged for shares in a company.

CONVERTIBLE PREFERRED SHARES: Dividend-paying shares that can also be exchanged for common shares at a predetermined price within a specified length of time.

CORRECTION: Refers to a stock or a market that is going down.

COUPON: The detachable part of a bond entitling the holder to a cash payment of the interest owning on a specific date.

CYCLICAL STOCK: A stock within a particular industry sector that is particularly sensitive to swings in economic conditions. They usually have strong results in a good economy and poor earnings when the economy weakens.

CURRENT ASSETS: Assets that are expected to be used up or converted to cash within the next year. Cash, accounts receivable, and inventory are the major assets usually included in this group.

CURRENT LIABILITIES: Liabilities that are due or will become due in the next year. They usually include trade accounts payable, bank loans, the current portion of long-term debt and taxes payable.

DAY ORDER: An order to buy or sell a security valid only for the day the order is given.

DEBENTURE: A bond not backed by a pledge of specific assets.

DEFERRED PROFIT-SHARING PLAN (DPSP): A plan where a portion of a company's profits is put into savings and investments to benefit employees.

DEFINED BENEFIT PENSION PLAN: A pension where the amount to be paid out at retirement is spelled out in advance.

DEPRECIATION: The drop in value of an asset due to age.

DERIVATIVE: This is a security whose value is derived from the underlying value of another security such as a stock, an index or commodity.

DISCOUNT: The amount by which a bond or note sells below par value.

DISCOUNT BROKER: This type of firm performs the services like that of a traditional brokerage firm, but does not offer investment advice to clients. These firms charge lower trading fees than the full-service brokers.

DIVIDEND: Cash paid on a regular basis to the owner of a stock by the company.

DIVIDEND REINVESTMENT: Some stocks and mutual fund companies allow dividends to be reinvested to purchase additional shares or units.

DIVIDEND YIELD: The annual dividend payment expressed as a percentage of the stock price.

DIVERSIFICATION: The technique of spreading your investment program over different investments, types of industries, companies and risks. This technique is used to minimize risks by making certain that not "all your eggs are in one basket."

DIVIDEND-INCOME FUND: A mutual fund where most of the investments are purchased because of the dividends they produce.

DOLLAR-COST AVERAGING: Averaging out the cost of purchasing units of an investment (e.g. stocks) by buying fixed amounts of the investment on a regular basis over a number of years.

DOW JONES INDUSTRIAL AVERAGE: The Dow Jones average of 30 industrials is the world's most widely followed stock market index and among the oldest (begun in 1896). It includes a selection of stocks that is considered representative of the breadth and reach of large business in the US.

EARNED INCOME: A technical term used by Revenue Canada to describe earnings from employment minus certain deductions

EARNINGS PER SHARE: Net income divided by the number of shares that a company has issued.

EITHER-OR: An order to buy one of two or more specified securities. When the order is executed, the others are canceled.

EQUITY FUNDS: Mutual funds that invest in common and preferred shares.

EXCESS CONTRIBUTIONS: RRSP contributions that exceed your annual limit and that cannot be claimed as a tax deduction.

EXTENDABLE BOND/DEBENTURE: The right of the issue to extend the date of maturity on a bond or debenture by a specified number of years.

FACE VALUE: The value of a bond or debenture that appears on its face. Usually this is the amount that is due on maturity.

FINANCIAL STATEMENTS: In the annual report, these are the audited financial results for the year, including a balance sheet, a statement of profit and loss, a statement of retained earnings and a set of notes that explain any unusual items in the reports.

FIXED INCOME INVESTMENT: An investment that offers a fixed, regular return.

FIXED INTEREST RATE: A predetermined interest rate that will not change over the duration of the loan.

FIXED TERM: A stipulated term of a contract.

FLOATING RATE PREFERRED SHARES: Preferred shares where the dividend rate moves up and down in relation to the prime rate (the interest rate banks charge to their best customers).

FLOOR TRADER: A brokerage firm employee who works on the stock exchange floor and is responsible to execute buy and sell orders on behalf of the firm's clients.

FRONT END LOADED MUTUAL FUND: A mutual fund where the sales commission is paid at the time of purchase.

FUTURE VALUE: The amount that an investment will be worth at some future time if it grows at a constant rate of interest.

FUTURES: A contract to buy or sell a commodity at a fixed price at a future date.

GAMBLING: The act of committing funds on the basis of tips, hunches or whims in the hope of realizing very large and quick gains.

GOLD BULLION: Large quantities of gold, usually in bar form.

GROSS UP OF DIVIDENDS: The process of taking the actual amount of dividends received from taxable Canadian corporations and increasing or "grossing up," the actual amount by 25 percent. This higher amount is added to your income and the Federal Dividend Tax Credit is then calculated on this higher amount.

GROWTH STOCK: A stock where added value is expected to come from a much higher share price in the future.

GUARANTEED INVESTMENT CERTIFICATE (GIC): A certificate issued by banks or trust companies that guarantees a set rate of return on an investment over a fixed period.

HEDGE: A means of protection against financial loss.

HIGH: The highest price at which a security trades, usually during a trading day unless otherwise specified.

HOLD: The level at which an investment is neither cheap enough to buy nor expensive enough to sell.

INCOME FUND: A mutual fund that purchases high-yield, low-risk investments.

INCOME STOCKS: These companies pay higher than average dividends.

INCOME SPLITTING: Splitting of one person's income with two or more people, usually for taxation purposes.

INCORPORATION: The establishment of a business as a legal entity.

INFLATION: The annual increase in the cost of living.

INSTALLMENT RECEIPTS: Usually accompany a new issue of securities, which allow the buyer to pay for the security in installments.

INSTITUTION: Usually refers to a buyer or seller of investments such as a pension fund, mutual fund or other large professional manager of money.

INTEREST: The rent paid on borrowed money.

INTEREST RATE: The agreed upon amount of rent to be paid for borrowing money.

INVESTING: The act of committing funds for a period of more than a year to a security after careful analysis of the risk and returns offered.

INVESTMENT PORTFOLIO: The collection of various kinds of investments held by an individual or a corporation.

I.P.O. This is an abbreviation for initial public offering. It refers to the first investment offering that a company makes to the buying public.

JUNIOR STOCK: A term for a small start-up company.

JUNK BOND: A high-risk, high-interest bond issued by a company usually in poor financial condition.

LARGE CAP: A company where the total dollar value of its shares is among the very largest.

LEVERAGE: The borrowing of money to buy something. The more money borrowed (compared to the amount of cash), the more "leveraged" the investment.

LIABILITIES: Money owed to someone else

LIMIT ORDER: An order to buy or sell securities at a price stipulated by the client, whereby the order can only be executed at the specified price or a better one.

LIQUIDITY: The ability of a market for a security to absorb a reasonable amount of buying or selling without major price changes and the ease with which an investment can be converted to cash.

LISTED AND UNLISTED STOCKS: Stocks that are listed are approved by trading by one or more of the stock exchanges. Stocks that are unlisted (or not listed for trading on an exchange) are traded "over-the-counter" between brokers. The unlisted market is sometimes called the "curb" market.

LOAD: A sales charge on each share or unit of a mutual fund. It covers the sales commissions paid to the broker or distribution company plus other administration and selling expenses. There are also "no-load" funds.

LONG-TERM (FIXED) ASSETS: Tangible assets of a long life (usually greater than a year), not intended for resale, and to be used in the operations of a business. Long-term assets include plant and equipment, but not inventories or accounts receivable.

LONG-TERM LIABILITIES: Liabilities that are not due in the next year. Long-term liabilities usually include bonds, debentures, mortgages, and similar types of debt.

LONG-TERM RETURN: Return on an investment over a long time.

MARGIN: The amount a company is willing to lend you against securities held as collateral.

MARGIN ACCOUNT: A brokerage account that allows the client to pay a portion of the price of the securities and borrow the balance from the broker. "Margin" is the difference between the market value of the stock and the loan that the broker makes against it.

MARGINAL TAX RATE: A combined rate (percentage) of income tax paid on the last (or next) dollar of taxable income. It is calculated as follows: Provincial (territorial) rate of tax x federal marginal rate of tax for tax bracket + federal marginal rate of tax.

MARGIN CALL: When the value of securities held as collateral against a loan drops below a fixed level, the borrower is required to come up with additional capital to cover the shortfall or risk having the securities covering the loan sold.

MARKETABILITY: The ease with which an investment can be bought or sold without seriously affecting its price. For example, "blue chip" stocks are usually highly marketable, since they are actively traded.

MARKET ORDER: An order to buy or sell securities immediately at the best possible price.

MATURITY: The date when money loaned or borrowed for an investment has to be paid back in full, with interest.

MID-CAP: A company where the total dollar value of its shares is mid-sized.

MONEY MARKET FUND: A mutual fund that purchases government and corporate interest-bearing investments, generally maturing in under one year.

MONEY PURCHASE PENSION PLAN: A pension plan whose value at retirement is based on the growth of the plan's investments. There are no guarantees as to the amount paid out at retirement.

MORTGAGE: Money borrowed from a financial institution to buy property.

MORTGAGE BACKED SECURITIES: Securities investing in first mortgages on residential properties.

MUTUAL FUND: A professionally managed company that invests large pools of capital on behalf of smaller investors.

MUTUAL FUND SWITCHING PRIVILEGES: These privileges allow an investor to switch out of or into a different fund(s) within the same family at very low or no commission.

NET WORTH: The value of things you own, minus the money you owe.

NO-LOAD MUTUAL FUND: A mutual fund where no fee is charged on the buying and selling of its units.

NET EARNINGS: The profits after all expenses and taxes are deducted.

NEW ISSUE: A stock or bond sold by a corporation for the first time. Proceeds may be used to retire outstanding securities of the company, for new plant or equipment, or for additional working capital. New debt issues are also offered by government bodies.

NO-LOAD FUND: A mutual fund where no sales or redemption charges are levied for buying or selling its units.

NO PAR VALUE: A description of a company's stock. Prior to 1917, the capital stocks of all companies in Canada had a par value. In that year the Dominion Companies Act permitted the issuance of stock without par value. The par value of a share of stock is usually of little significance compared with the book value and the market value.

ODD LOT: An amount of stock less than the 100 share round lot.

OFFER: The price at which an investor can buy a security.

OPEN-ENDED MUTUAL FUND: A mutual fund that buys its units back directly from its investors.

OPEN ORDER: A "good till canceled" order.

OPTION: A stock market "bet" that a particular investment will rise or fall in value over a short period of time.

OPTION FUND: A mutual fund that invests in options.

OVER BOUGHT: A market where excessive buying has pushed prices too high.

OVER SOLD: A market where excessive selling has pushed prices too low.

OVER THE COUNTER: These securities are not listed on one of the exchanges.

OVERWEIGHT: To raise the percentage of one's portfolio exposed to a particular type of investment.

PAR (OR FACE) VALUE: The amount returned to bondholders at maturity. The stated face value of a bond or stock as assigned by the company's charter and expressed as dollars and cents per share. Par value of a common stock usually has little relationship to the current market value and so "no par value" stock is now the norm. Par value of a preferred stock is significant as it indicates the dollar amount of assets each preferred share would be entitled to in the event of winding up the company.

PENNY STOCKS: Shares that are usually valued at less than $1.

PORTABILITY: The ability to take the benefits promised by one company's pension plan and switch them to a second company's plan, or another approved plan such as an RRSP, when changing jobs.

PORTFOLIO: A group of securities held or owned for investment purposes by an individual or institutional investor. An investor's portfolio may contain common and preferred shares, bonds, options, and other types of securities.

PRECIOUS METALS: Metals mined for their monetary rather than their manufacturing value.

PRECIOUS METAL FUND: A mutual fund that invests in precious metals.

PREFERRED SHARE: A kind of share that pays an annual return, or dividend, and has priority over the common shareholder should the company go bankrupt.

PRICE EARNINGS RATIO (P.E.): This is calculated by dividing a company's earnings per share by its stock price.

PRINCIPAL: The actual amount of money owing on a mortgage or a loan, not including the interest.

PRIVATE COMPANY: A company whose shares are not traded on a stock market.

PROMISSORY NOTE: A written promise to repay borrowed money.

PROMOTER: Someone who hopes to profit from promoting the virtues of an investment.

PROSPECTUS: A legal document describing a new issue of securities for sale to the public, which is prepared in accordance with provincial securities commission regulations. A mutual fund prospectus contains information regarding the fund's investment objectives and restrictions, management fees, tax considerations and all other details pertinent to the fund.

PUBLIC COMPANY: A company whose shares are traded on a stock exchange.

PUT OPTION: A speculative investment, a bet that a stock, bond, or other financial vehicle will fall in value.

PUT: An option to sell a specified stock or security within a specified time period for a specified price.

RALLY: Refers to a stock or market that is going up.

RATE OF RETURN: The amount of profit to be made on an investment, usually expressed as a percentage of the original amount.

REAL ESTATE INVESTMENT TRUST (REIT): An investment trust that holds a combination of real estate assets, including mortgages and property.

REBALANCE: To change the asset mix of a portfolio.

RESISTANCE: The top level of a price range that a stock or market will probably not rise above.

REGISTERED EDUCATION SAVINGS PLAN (RESP): A government registered savings plan that, if used for the future post secondary education of a child, offers some tax advantages.

REGISTERED PENSION PLAN: A government registered plan where both the employer and employee contribute to the employee's retirement fund.

REGISTERED RETIREMENT INCOME FUND (RRIF): Government registered accounts with financial institutions, into which people can, subject to certain conditions, transfer RRSP funds. These transferred funds are not taxed until withdrawn from the plan.

REGISTERED RETIREMENT SAVINGS PLANS (RRSP or RSP): A government registered account with any financial institution that allows money to be set aside and not taxed until it is withdrawn from the account, usually upon retirement.

RETRACTABLE BOND/DEBENTURE: A bond or debenture where the purchaser has the option of cashing in the bond or debenture at a previously agreed-upon price and time.

RETURN: The amount of income, in dollars, you receive from an investment.

RIGHTS: An investment that gives the holder the ability to buy a stock at a fixed price for a very short time, e.g. one month. Rights are usually offered to shareholders already holding stock in the company.

ROYALTY TRUSTS: An investment trust that gets income from royalties, with the most common form of income derived from owning a stake in an oil or gas well.

RUNAWAY INFLATION: When the cost of living dramatically increases every year.

SHORT SELLING: A stock market trading technique that can create a profit from the drop in the price of a stock.

SMALL CAP: A company where the dollar value of all its shares is very small.

SPECULATING: The act of committing funds for a short period of time and at high risks, in the hope of realizing large capital gains.

SPECULATIVE INVESTMENTS: Investments that come with both a high risk of losing your money, and the possibility of earning a high rate of return.

SPREAD: The difference in price between what a buyer is willing to pay and a seller is willing to receive for a specific investment.

STANDARD & POOR'S 500 (S&P 500): The Standard & Poor's index of 500 stocks is a broad measure of stock market performance and includes shares of most of the large public companies in the US.

STOCK/SHARES: Certificates representing ownership in a company.

STOCK MARKET: A financial marketplace where most types of investments can be bought and sold.

STOCK SPLIT: The division of a company's existing stock into more shares, with the approval of the shareholders. This is often done to reduce the price per share in order to improve the marketability of the shares.

STOP LOSS: An order to sell an investment if it drops below a predetermined price.

STRIP COUPON: An interest coupon that is physically separated from a bond; it can be bought and sold as a separate investment and promises a certain return to maturity. Strip coupons can be bought and sold before they come due.

SUPPORT: The bottom level of a price range that a stock or market will probably not go below.

TAX: Money collected by the government

TAX DEFERRAL: Paying taxeson money earned at a future date, rather than in the current calendar year.

TAXABLE INCOME: Income that Revenue Canada considers taxable.

TAXATION: The compulsory payment of money to a government.

TAX SHELTER: An investment, that by government regulation, can be made with untaxed or partly taxed dollars. The purpose of a tax shelter is to offset an individual's taxable income from other sources and thereby reduce tax liability.

TERM: A fixed period of time, usually in relationship to the payment of money.

TERM DEPOSITS: An investment that earns a fixed rate of return over a fixed time period.

TIPs 35: A derivative index participation unit linked to a diversified portfolio of 35 companies on the Toronto Stock Exchange 35 index.

TIPs 100: A derivative index participation unit traded on the Toronto Stock Exchange and linked to the TSE 100 index.

TORONTO 35: An index of 35 blue chip stocks on the Toronto Stock Exchange which includes most of the big Canadian companies across the major industry sectors.

TRADER: Anyone who buys and sell securities on a regular and frequent basis, whether a professional or amateur investor.

TRADES: Orders to buy and sell stocks

TREASURY BILLS: A form of short-term borrowing by the federal government from institutional lenders.

TSE 300: An index of the shares of 300 largest companies listed on the Toronto Stock Exchange.

UNDERWEIGHT: To lower the percentage of one's portfolio exposed to a particular type of investment.

UNDERWRITTEN: A security issue that an investment dealer has agreed to buy, in whole or in part, for resale to its clients. The company issuing the securities thus knows in advance how much money it will receive from the issue.

UNDERWRITER: Usually an investment dealer who agrees to buy all or part of a new security issue from a company, raising the money in the expectation that the securities can be resold to the public at a slightly higher price.

VARIABLE INTEREST RATE: A loan where the interest rate fluctuates in accordance with market conditions.

VARIABLE RETURN INVESTMENTS: Investments offering no set pattern of return. This includes any investment that does not carry a specified rate of return, such as common shares, real estate, etc.

VOLATILITY: Volatility is a measure of the rate of change in the price of a security over a specified time. The usual yardstick is standard deviation from average price.

VOLUME: The number of security units traded during a specified period. With stocks it is the number of shares; with bond and currencies it is the value; and with derivatives, such as futures and options, it is the number of contracts.

WARRANT: The option to buy a stock at a fixed price over a set period of time, usually issued to "sweeten" the sale of new stock.

WINDFALL PROFIT: Profit that comes swifty and unexpectedly.

YIELD: The amount of interest or dividend paid on a loan or an investment, expressed as a percentage. The yield on a stock is calculated by dividing the dividend by the current market price. This is also called the rate of return.

INDEX